University ~~ter~~

BLOOMSBURY AND THE
DECORATIVE ARTS

Omega and after

BLOOMSBURY AND THE DECORATIVE ARTS

ISABELLE ANSCOMBE

photographs by Howard Grey

WITH 124 ILLUSTRATIONS, 20 IN COLOUR

Foreword by JOHN LEHMANN

Thames and Hudson

Frontispiece Wooden signboard, painted by Duncan Grant in May 1915, which used to hang outside the Omega Workshops at 33 Fitzroy Square, London.

© 1981 Isabelle Anscombe and Howard Grey
Foreword © 1981 Thames and Hudson Ltd, London
First paperback edition 1984
Reprinted 1989

Printed and bound in the German Democratic Republic

0500233373

19133723

Contents

FOREWORD

by John Lehmann

Most people, when they hear the name Bloomsbury, think first of the novels of Virginia Woolf, the de-bunking historical writings of Lytton Strachey, and perhaps also of the novels of E. M. Forster. The dominance of the literary side in people's minds certainly continued all through the inter-war years; in spite of the fact that the inner nucleus of Bloomsbury contained two highly individual artists and two controversial art critics. It is only recently, it seems to me, that the importance of the visual side of Bloomsbury has begun to be recognized, and the rare gifts of Vanessa Bell and Duncan Grant and the significance they had in breaking down the artistic conventions of their time in England are now accepted in a wider world beyond the circle of devoted admirers they always had.

During the first quarter of the present century a minor revolution took place in the English artistic world, and I think one can say with little qualification that the instigator and animating spirit behind that revolution was a late-comer to Bloomsbury, the painter and art critic Roger Fry. It was he who was captivated by the innovating developments that were taking place in the artistic world of Paris in the years immediately before the First World War, and decided that the English must get to know of them and be subjected to their influence. It was from the new atmosphere created by his second Post-Impressionist Exhibition that Roger Fry, bubbling with theories and projects as ever, conceived the idea of the Omega Workshops. I need not go into the history of the project, which is all admirably expounded in the present work, except to say that it resulted in an explosion of the decorative arts that had not been seen in this country since the movement led by William Morris in the previous century. Roger Fry believed that young artists should be able to earn a living not merely by the always chancy sale of their canvases, but by interior decoration and the designing of objects, tables, chairs, jugs, bowls, vases and boxes to harmonize with wall-paintings, curtains and soft furnishings specially created for a novel and stimulating total effect.

The project started, splendidly enough, in the summer of 1913, and was patronized not only by enthusiastic followers of Bloomsbury but also by influential hostesses and social figures. The bad luck that pursued it was caused partly by the First World War that broke out a year later, but also by dissension among the artists Fry had persuaded to take part in it.

The Omega Workshops, in spite of the energy Fry expended in keeping them going, were closed six years later. I was too young to visit the Omega during the brief span of their existence, but in the late twenties and thirties I had many friends in Bloomsbury and among its adherents, and in their houses and studios I could see an abundance of enchanting designs from the circle of Vanessa Bell and Duncan Grant. Above all the wall-paintings, chiefly by those two artists: they filled the rooms with their marvellous light and colour and the sinuous, sensual curves of the figures depicted in them. Many of these were destroyed in the bombings of the Second War, but some survived, especially in the country, to delight us still and to remind us of the inspiration from which they were born.

The spirit of Omega did not die entirely. It was revived in part when the London Artists' Association was created, under the tutelage of Maynard Keynes, in the mid-twenties. The Association had the excellent idea of putting on a Christmas show every year, where one could buy not only paintings by the artists who were members – and many were the same as those who had contributed to the Omega Workshops – but also objects created and painted by these artists, jugs, vases, trays, match-box holders, teacups and saucers, all delightful to look at and to handle, and to solve many a Christmas present problem. Like many others, I found it a joy to wander through the galleries, tempted at every step by what I saw. I must confess that though the choosing of presents was my intention, some of the purchases I made never got beyond my own flat; and are still in my possession to be gloated over.

How sad it is that a younger generation has not had the will, or the interest, to revive such decorative activities once more: now plainness is all.

Preface

Duncan Grant and Vanessa Bell seem to me to have been enigmatic artists. To themselves and to the critics they were first and foremost canvas painters, yet their decorative work shows a far more remarkable talent. At Charleston one looks past the paintings on the walls to the walls themselves.

First of all the eye is attracted to the colours which Duncan and Vanessa employed. In decorating they used a distinctive and highly sophisticated palette which they seldom fully exploited on canvas. The strong colours of the Omega period were borrowed from French Post-Impressionism, but later, during the 1920s, they perfected a technique of justaposing a limited selection of softer colours which is unique.

Secondly their decorations are based on an elaboration of handwriting: they used devices peculiar to themselves as design elements which could be built up in any configuration to cover an allotted space. The coherence of such an alphabet allowed them to decorate almost anything without incongruity, and a profusion of decorated objects could co-exist harmoniously, whether designed by Duncan in 1920 or by Vanessa in 1950.

Their technique excluded much that other designers take for granted and demonstrated a particular type of restraint: they refused to add flourishes, cared little for a virtuoso performance of care and finish and were not out to impress by their originality, nor by being smart in a fashionable sense. Their manner of embellishing an interior is without precedent in British decorative traditions.

The sheer amount of design work which they undertook shows that they enjoyed it. Was this just a habit formed at the Omega or did they realize that in decorating they could achieve something which seemed to elude them on canvas?

An original artistic sense is equally apparent in their photographs. There are well over a thousand negatives taken by Vanessa, Duncan and their family and friends over a period of about sixty years. Visually these pictures form a remarkable collection of family photography. In most of them one is aware that the photographer (generally Vanessa) was less concerned with focus and exposure than with composition, rendering the collection casual but highly artistic. The event of taking a picture was apparently considered more important than the attention given to the processes involved, an attitude which is ultimately beneficial to photography.

H.G.

Roger Fry and the foundation of the Omega Workshops

THE Omega Workshops Ltd were started in London in 1913 by Roger Fry, with the painters Vanessa Bell and Duncan Grant as his co-directors. They were not allied in any way to the Arts and Crafts Movement of the 1870s and 1880s, and their closest model was probably the Wiener Werkstätte, a decorative arts workshop started in 1903 by the artists and architects of the Vienna Secession. The Omega brought together many young English artists interested in the work of the French Post-Impressionists and gave them both a meeting place and a means of livelihood at a time when patronage was scarce. The artists decorated and designed fabrics, furniture, pottery and many smaller items which were sold from premises in Fitzroy Square, giving them a small but regular income.

In 1910 Roger Fry, at the age of forty-four, had returned to London from New York where for four years he had been curator and then adviser of the Department of Paintings at the Metropolitan Museum. As a student at Cambridge Fry had read natural sciences, but soon afterwards he turned to art criticism. His main interest was in Italian Renaissance painting, especially the work of Giotto and Cimabue, and his first book, published in 1899, was on Giovanni Bellini. He was respected in the art world as an expert whose opinion conferred a seal of authenticity and for four years he had enjoyed the benefits of being the representative of such a wealthy institution as the Met, travelling extensively in Europe in search of acquisitions for the Museum. By 1910, however, a conflict of interests had arisen between the Museum and one of its directors, the influential and baronial J. Pierpont Morgan, over the purchase of a Fra Angelico in Paris, and Fry came to realize that his expertise and his adoration of art were principally exploitable commodities in an expanding market. He resigned and returned, jobless, to London.

Fry had turned down the Directorship of the National Gallery in London in 1906 because he had already agreed to go to New York and he now declined the Directorship of the Tate Gallery, mainly for financial reasons; but he failed to gain the Slade Professorship at Cambridge on which he had pinned his hopes. This left him dependent on his writing, and he contributed articles to *The Athenaeum* and *The Burlington Magazine* on subjects as diverse as Italian painting, Chinese ceramics, Islamic art, Albrecht Dürer and modern sculpture. Gradually he developed an appreciation of modern painting. In 1908, after an International Society Exhibition which included Matisse and Gauguin, he had written in *The Burlington Magazine*:

> Two other artists, MM. Cézanne and Paul Gauguin, are not really Impression-ists at all. They are proto-Byzantines rather than neo-Impressionists . . . There is no need for me to praise Cézanne – his position is already assured – but if one compares his still-life . . . with Monet's, I think it will be admitted that it marks a great advance in intellectual content. It leaves far less to the casual dictation of natural appearance. The relations of every tone and colour are deliberately chosen and stated in unmistakable terms. In the placing of objects, in the relation of one form to another, in the values of colour which indicate mass, and in the purely decorative elements of design, Cézanne's work seems to me to betray a finer, more scrupulous artistic sense.[1]

He now began to trace the qualities he found in Cézanne and Matisse in much earlier painters, especially Masaccio and Signorelli, and by 1911 was writing of a 'surprisingly modern Virgin and Child' by Masaccio included in an exhibition at the Grafton Galleries:

> What is common to most Florentine design, and what is hardly found out of Florence, is here raised to its highest efficiency – perfect plastic synthesis of the design, its extraordinary compression and its intellectual lucidity. It is through the compression of these ample forms within the picture space, through the apprehended effect of momentum in their large and simple gestures, that the mysterious significance of the whole appears.[2]

He could as well be describing a Matisse. It was with the new terms by which he analysed paintings – key words such as 'design', 'mass', 'colour' and 'significance' – that he began to build a coherent theory of aesthetics.

On his return home Fry had also faced a personal tragedy. His wife Helen had had bouts of recurring mental illness since 1898, only two years after their marriage, and was now declared incurably insane. She was unable to live with him again. Fry was left with two young children and a new house, Durbins, in Guildford, which had been completed to his designs only the previous year. Despite his sorrow and disillusionment, he was able to write to G. L. Dickinson, one of his closest friends, in September of that year: 'I've given up even regretting the callus that had to form to let me go through with things. Now and again it gives and I could cry for the utter pity and wastefulness of things, but life is too urgent ...'[3] For Fry the urgency of life still lay in art and he was prepared to risk even his reputation, on which he depended to earn a living, in championing an art in which he now passionately believed.

The Grafton Galleries offered Fry the use of their facilities during the autumn months and in November 1910 he organized an exhibition, 'Manet and the Post-Impressionists', which rocked London art circles. It included works by Cézanne, Van Gogh, Gauguin, Matisse, Picasso, Derain, Seurat, Rouault and others. The reaction was swift and decided. The paintings were the work of 'pavement pastellists', 'a jest', or 'the crude efforts of children'. In his diary Wilfrid Blunt expressed the view that the exhibition was nothing but 'that gross puerility which scrawls indecencies on the walls of a privy, a pornographic show'.

What probably shocked the critics as much as anything was that Fry's theories found close affinities between the then valueless canvases of the Post-Impressionists and the treasured frescoes of the Italian Renaissance. Ten years later, in the 'Retrospect' to *Vision and Design*, he was able to sum up the motives behind such scandalized reviews:

> I now see that my crime had been to strike at the vested emotional interests. These people felt instinctively that their special culture was one of their social assets. That to be able to speak glibly of T'ang and Ming, of Amico di Sandro [an invention of Bernard Berenson's] and Baldovinetti, gave them a social standing and a distinctive *cachet*. This showed me that we had all along been labouring under a mutual misunderstanding, i.e. that we have admired the Italian primitives for quite different reasons.[4]

As a result of this exhibition Fry forfeited the protection of the respectable art world, but he found many new friends among young artists who were excited by Post-Impressionism. He had renewed a rather cursory acquaintance with the art critic Clive Bell and his wife Vanessa. Clive, fifteen years Roger's junior, already had an interest in French painting, having lived in Paris after graduating from Cambridge, and he accompanied Roger to Paris to choose works for the Manet show. Vanessa was an artist who could share Roger's own passion for painting. At this time Roger also met Duncan Grant, Frederick Etchells and Wyndham Lewis, all of whom were in their twenties and were familiar with the most recent French innovations: Etchells had met Picasso, Braque and Modigliani in Paris when he had a studio there, and Grant and Lewis had first met in Paris in 1907. Roger became a pivotal figure within a group of artists who wanted to explore the new forms of expression in their own work.

Vanessa later wrote that, although she admired the work of the English painters who belonged to the New English Art Club, it gave her no sense of direction. She had been attracted by the few canvases and reproductions of Cézanne, Pissarro and Van Gogh that she had seen, but it was the Manet exhibition which, in a riot of colour and new appreciation of form, confirmed her excitement. According to Duncan Grant, 'It was really a moment which brought together all the younger painters in England into a sort of mass movement. They agreed that something had happened that they must cope with and I think that is what led eventually to the Omega.'[5]

Roger began to spend more time at 46 Gordon Square, the Bells' house in London, and in April 1911, after the outcry at the exhibition had died down, he travelled with them, and another Cambridge friend, Harry Norton, to Constantinople and on through Turkey. At Brusa Vanessa suffered a miscarriage and it was Roger who nursed her and accompanied her home. During this time they realized that they were in love with each other.

Vanessa was then a resplendent woman of thirty-one. Her brother-in-law, Leonard Woolf, described her as possessing a goddess-like physical splendour, and went on to say that

> To many people she appeared frightening and formidable. . . . I myself never found her formidable, partly because she had the most beautiful speaking voice that I have ever heard, and partly because of her tranquillity and quietude. (The tranquillity was to some extent superficial; it did not extend deep down in her mind, for there in the depths there was also an extreme sensitivity, a nervous tension . . .)[6]

Vanessa was tall with a stately figure, hair tied up at the back of her head, and heavy-lidded eyes, which accentuated the calm of her demeanour. She was not a woman who suffered fools gladly but at the same time she was shy, a combination which many friends and acquaintances, especially those younger than she, could occasionally take for disdain. She had been married for four years to Clive Bell, who came from a wealthy coal-owning family whose principal pursuits were sports and hunting. They had two children, Julian, who was three, and Quentin, who had been born the previous summer.

Roger probably loved Vanessa more than any other woman in his life. After the crushing disappointments of his return from New York, he was now full of hope and plans. He was in love, he was at the centre of a group of people who shared his enthusiasms, and there was much that he could do practically to help them. He quickly followed up the initial onslaught of the Manet exhibition.

In June 1911 he was commissioned by an old friend, Basil Williams, to decorate the students' dining hall at Borough Polytechnic in London and he invited his friends to join him in executing the scheme. Murals were planned on the theme of 'London on Holiday'. Fry, Grant, Etchells, Bernard Adeney, Albert Rutherston and Macdonald Gill painted scenes entitled *Punch and Judy, Football, Bathing, The Zoo, The Fair, Toy Sailing Boats* and *Paddlers*, which are now in the Tate Gallery. Roger encouraged the others to experiment with a mosaic technique in laying on the colour, following the ideas he had conceived after seeing mosaics in Constantinople. He had earlier called the Post-Impressionists 'proto-Byzantines' and felt that the delineation of colour and form in mosaic was closely allied to Cézanne's use of blocks of colour.

In July the next year he again joined forces with Grant and Etchells when he organized an exhibition of English artists in Paris, at the Galerie Barbazanges in the rue Saint-Honoré. The Exposition de Quelques Artistes Indépendants Anglais also included work by Vanessa Bell, Etchells' sister Jessie, Wyndham Lewis, Spencer Gore, C. J. Holmes and Charles Ginner. At this time Roger must have visited the Atelier Martine, as the Galerie Barbazanges was at 109 rue Saint-Honoré and the Martine, which had opened in April 1911, was at 107.

The Martine was started by the Paris couturier Paul Poiret, who had been a pupil of Jacques Doucet, one of the first collectors of modern French art and decorative design. Poiret had visited the Wiener Werkstätte and also the Palais Stoclet in Brussels, designed by Josef Hoffmann, and although he disliked the rigidity of their doctrines he greatly admired the new spirit in the work of Hoffmann, Kolo Moser and Gustav Klimt. On his return he decided to do something similar himself, but in a way that would encourage the free creativity he admired.

Poiret gathered fifteen teenage girls of working-class background from the municipal grammar schools, paid them a small wage and provided two meals a day. He took them to the zoo, the aquarium, the marketplaces, the Paris hothouses and the Sèvres manufactory and then left them, with no formal training, to transcribe their impressions in terms of designs for fabrics, painted pottery, murals and painted furniture. Artist friends of Poiret, including Matisse, Dufy, Segonzac and Van Dongen, frequently visited the Martine. Poiret also set up a workshop in the Boulevard de Clichy for Raoul Dufy to handblock fabrics, and the girls were often taken there to assist. In 1912 Dufy accepted a better offer from Bianchini-Ferrier in Lyons, but Poiret continued to buy and use his fabrics.

The venture proved so successful that Poiret opened an interior decoration business at 831 rue Saint-Honoré, selling fabrics, embroideries, wall-papers, screens, panels, an assortment of china and pottery and rugs from the Martine, as well as offering a decorating service for private commissions, which included such famous patrons as Isadora Duncan. In 1912 the Martine showed two rooms of sketches, patterns, curtains and wall panels at the Salon d'Automne and exhibited rugs at the Galerie Barbazanges, which also showed the work of Sonia Delaunay and Marie Laurencin. The Martine successfully incorporated not only the ideas of the Wiener Werkstätte and of Post-Impressionism, but also the startling colours of Bakst's designs for the Ballets Russes, which came to Paris in May 1909.

Roger's plans for some kind of artists' organization began early in 1912. In February he wrote to Wyndham Lewis asking him to a meeting at Vanessa's house to discuss the nature of a group which they planned to start with Grant and Etchells: this could have been either the Omega or the Grafton Group of painters, which Roger founded in 1913 with the intention of exhibiting the work of artists he admired. Vanessa had founded a discussion group for fellow artists in 1905, called the Friday Club, which exhibited annually. Most of its members were women, although both Duncan Grant and Henry Lamb had put in an appearance. Roger was concerned by the poverty of many of the young artists and wanted to find some practical means of help. It may well have been the Atelier Martine which inspired the idea of opening a workshop. In a letter to Bernard Shaw in December explaining his plans, Roger wrote,

Already in France Poiret's Ecole Martine shows what delightful new possibilities are revealed in this direction, what added gaiety and charm their products give to an interior. My workshop would be carried on on similar lines and might probably work in conjunction with the Ecole Martine, by mutual exchange of ideas and products. I have also the promise of assistance from several young French artists who have had experience of such work: but in the main I wish to develop a definitely English tradition.[7]

Poiret certainly wanted to expand his ideas outside the boundaries of France, but it is uncertain whether these plans would have amounted to anything even if the war had not intervened. Although Roger had great confidence in his English artists, the Omega would undoubtedly have benefited from closer contact with developments in France.

Vanessa had already expressed her doubts about the inherent strength of the English tradition. During the summer of 1912 she and Clive had gone to stay with Clive's parents at Seend in Wiltshire. The atmosphere there, which always depressed her by its wealthy tastelessness, perhaps brought home to her the sheer impossibility of ever influencing such people to appreciate art. On their way to Seend the Bells had stopped to join Roger and his friend Henri Doucet at Newington, where they were staying with the artists Ethel Sands and Nan Hudson, probably with a view to discussing their inclusion in the plans for the Omega. The seventeenth-century house at Newington was decorated with chintzes and pale silks in tones of grey, green and white, with carefully placed bowls of rose and violet flowers, all arranged like a still life. From Seend Vanessa wrote to Roger with ruthless honesty explaining her distress at the problems which, she now realized, faced their plans:

Clive said he couldn't stand Newington and was thankful to get to Seend where at least we could be 'jolly'. I own I'm degenerate enough to prefer the refined Ethel and Nan – where at any rate one can enjoy free talk. All the same I was a little alarmed at their excessive elegance and 18th century stamp. It isn't what we want even for our minor arts, is it? Won't they import too much of that? Of course I know they're useful, but don't you think we shall have to be careful, especially in England where it seems to me one can never get away from all this fatal prettiness. Can't we paint stuffs etc. which won't be gay and pretty? I see how easy it would be to turn out yards of very fanciful and light and piquant things and I don't see what else that couple can do. I daresay you're right in using them, but although I don't go to Clive's lengths, I must say that seeing them in their chosen surroundings did give us rather the creeps, at least when I thought of turning that into anything to do with art. Does that sound priggish?[8]

The Omega did not eventually include the two artists, although Ethel Sands later commissioned the Workshops to decorate her Chelsea flat.

In October 1912 Roger organized the Second Post-Impressionist Exhibition at the Grafton Galleries. He selected the French work, Boris Anrep the Russian and Clive Bell the English, which included paintings by Duncan Grant, Vanessa Bell, Frederick Etchells, Wyndham Lewis, Stanley Spencer, Henry Lamb, Bernard Adeney and Spencer Gore and sculpture by Eric Gill. This exhibition gave Roger a further chance to clarify his aesthetic theories. Ten years earlier he had admonished a New English Art Club exhibition for its dependence on representation:

> The arbitrary rule that they have formulated is that they may leave out anything they like in a given scene, but that they must not introduce forms which do not happen to be there, however much these might increase the harmony or intensify the idea.[9]

He had now arrived at a more definite statement of what he felt the aesthetically satisfying elements of art to be. The experiences of life were to be transformed in the artist's mind into a significant grouping of mass and colour, and it was therefore in the design of a picture that the full force of the artist's vision communicated itself. In the catalogue to the Second Post-Impressionist Exhibition, Roger wrote:

> Now these artists do not seek to give what can, after all, be but a pale reflex of actual appearance, but to arouse the conviction of a new and definite reality. They do not seek to imitate form, but to create form, not to imitate life, but to find an equivalent for life. By that I mean that they wish to make images which by the clearness of their logical structure, and by their closely-knit unity of texture, shall appeal to our disinterested and contemplative imagination with something of the same vividness as the things of actual life appeal to our practical activities. In fact they aim not at illusion but at reality.[10]

Roger Fry aroused great antagonism among the other critics and painters of his generation by upholding the supremacy of form over narrative content. William Rothenstein, who declined an offer to exhibit with the Omega, was still arguing the point twenty years later, in the chapter 'A Post-Impressionist Exhibition' in his book *Men and Memories*: 'Art and literature which do not combine form with human drama cannot satisfy mankind . . . Interest in form for its own sake has never distinguished English painters.'[11]

At the end of 1912 prospectuses were sent out with the aim of raising money to start the Omega. Clive Bell, Bernard Shaw, Hugh Lane, Sir Ian

1 Firescreen designed by Duncan Grant and embroidered by Lady Ottoline Morrell in 1912; at least two other versions were made for the Omega.

II *Painted screen by Duncan Grant shown at the Omega opening in July 1913, and now at Charleston (see pl. XIX). On the left are a cast of the ears of Michelangelo's 'David', a portrait of Adrian Stephen by Duncan, and a photograph of Vanessa Bell.*

III *Silk fan and two boxes painted by Duncan Grant for the Omega, c.1913.*

IV *Painted Omega dining table by Roger Fry, c.1913.*

V *Painted Omega metal tray by Edward Wolfe, c.1918.*

VI *Log box at Charleston painted by Duncan Grant, c.1916.*

VII 'Amenophis',
printed linen designed by
Roger Fry for the Omega
in 1913.

VIII Bowl thrown by
Quentin Bell and
decorated by Vanessa
Bell, 1940s.

IX Vase thrown by
Quentin Bell and
decorated by Duncan
Grant, 1940s.

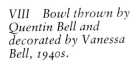

X Vase cast by Phyllis Keyes and decorated by Duncan Grant in the 1930s, standing on a tiled table made for Leonard and Virginia Woolf in the late 1920s.

XI Tiled fireplace surround at Monks House, Sussex, painted for Leonard and Virginia Woolf, probably by Vanessa Bell, c.1931.

and Lady Hamilton and Sir Kay Muir, Lady Hamilton's brother, all contributed and Roger was to continue to support the Omega with a legacy from his uncle Joseph. Clive Bell's father, however, declined, 'saying that the project would have appealed to him very much if he had not been to the Grafton, but that after going there he was afraid he would have nothing to do with it'.[12] Nevertheless, by February 1913 Roger had amassed £1,500 of the £2,000 he had hoped for and work began.

In the new year Etchells wrote to Vanessa that he expected to come to London and find paid work for decoration immediately. Some Omega products were shown in February and March at the Second Post-Impressionist Exhibition held at the Sandon Society in Liverpool, where Roger went to lecture during the show. A screen by Grant and a painted table by Etchells were included in the first Grafton Group exhibition at the Alpine Club Gallery in London in March, which included paintings, shown anonymously, by Fry, Grant, Bell, Lewis and Etchells, the founder members of the Omega.

The Omega Workshops were registered as a company on 14 May 1913 and premises were taken at 33 Fitzroy Square in Bloomsbury, not far from the Tottenham Court Road. Roger was responsible for all the practical side of setting up the business and was never so happy as when impossibly busy. His first flush of enthusiasm was founded on his faith in the talent of the artists he had gathered around him. He told G. L. Dickinson:

> It needs a tremendous lot of work to organize it properly. The artists are delightful people but ever so impractical. When I think of how practical the French artists are, I almost wish these weren't the delightful, vague, impossible Englishmen that they are. But I think I can manage them and it's very exciting . . . The artists have a tremendous lot of invention and a new feeling for colour and proportion that astonishes me. My fearful problem is to harness the forces I've got and to get the best out of them practically, and it's the deuce to do. I have to think out all between the design and the finished product and how to sell it; also how to pay the artists, and it's almost more than I can manage. However, I hope I shall get it through. Also I have to be bagman: I go out into smart society and advertise my scheme.[13]

To his mother, Lady Fry, he wrote:

> My Omega Workshops are hard at work and keep me at it pretty continuously. There's a great deal of interest shown everywhere in the scheme and I hope I may be able to pull it through. If I do I shall I think have done something to make art possible in England. It would be of course almost to accomplish a

OMEGA WORKSHOPS Ltd
ARTIST DECORATORS

| TELEPHONE, 3331 REGENT | 33 FITZROY SQ. LONDON W. |

From an undated catalogue of the Omega Workshops.

miracle, but I have hopes. Certainly the people I have got have an extraordinary amount of talent. My problem is how to harness it to practical purposes. There's no doubt that it is a difficult thing to do and perhaps that is why almost all manufacturers give it up and go to the patient hack instead of the artist for their designs.[14]

In addition to the artists of the Grafton Group – Fry, Grant, Bell, Etchells and Lewis – up to twenty others found employment at the Workshops at various times. Some, like Henri Gaudier-Brzeska, sold their work through the Omega; others, like the American E. McKnight Kauffer or the textile designer Phyllis Barron, sometimes exhibited there but never became involved in the business. Paul Nash, David Bomberg, William Roberts and Mark Gertler all had connections with the Omega. In the early days the regular artists were Cuthbert Hamilton, a contemporary of Lewis's from the Slade; Edward Wadsworth, who had abandoned engineering to study painting; Etchells' beautiful sister Jessie; the French painter Henri Doucet; Jock Turnbull, who left to join the Territorial Army in July 1914 and returned shell-shocked a year later; Nina Hamnett, spontaneous and freedom-loving, but hard-working; and her husband Roald Kristian, who was also known as Edgar de Bergen. Three women from the Slade helped to run the place – Barbara Bagenal (née Hiles), Gladys Hines and Winifred Gill, who had been secretary to Roger's sister Joan at Guildford. The group grew somewhat at random: Winnie Gill later wrote of Jock Turnbull, 'I don't remember when he joined us or where he came from. I expect he just walked in with a few drawings under his arm, like so many, and asked if he could be taken on. Sometimes Roger would politely refuse them, always a difficult thing to do.'[15]

The artists were not allowed to work at the Omega more than three and a half days a week, so that they would not be distracted from their more serious work, and for this they were paid 30s. per week or 7s. 6d. per day, although Winifred Gill received only 25s. per week. All the work at the Omega was sold anonymously, which guaranteed that no one artist would be especially sought after or earn more than the others.

Various other staff were also employed. There was a caretaker, Mr Miles, and a manager, Charles Robinson. During the war Mr Robinson went, as a conscientious objector, to join a Quaker mission in Corsica and then Winifred Gill took over until the beginning of 1917, when she left because she could no longer support herself on her salary. A retired house-painter, George Darling, was hired to prepare the surfaces of the furniture for painting. Ian Maxwell used to go and measure up for clients who ordered carpets, tables or other decorations, until he left for the war, where he was killed in action. There were others with differing connections with the Workshops: John Hope Johnston used to send packages of coloured silk squares and beautiful blue beads from the Near East and clay figures from North Africa. In later years Margery Shearer ran the showroom and helped to organize the Omega Club evenings with her friend Isabel Monk. At one time the women, Jessie, Nina, Winnie and Gladys, had a little girl apprentice to help them.

The official opening of the Omega Workshops took place on 8 July and received cautiously enthusiastic reviews. *The Times* liked the flat designs, presumably of the fabrics, but found the painted tables 'irrational'. Wishing the venture success, the critic summed up:

> But what pleases us most about all the work of these artists is its gaiety. They seemed to have worked, not sadly or conscientiously upon some artistic principle, but because they enjoyed doing so. They are not pharisaically or aggressively artistic, but in doing what they like themselves they have managed to forget all the bad art they do not like.[16]

No. 33 Fitzroy Square was a tall, terraced Georgian house. In 1915 a signboard painted by Duncan Grant was hung outside, with the Greek letter omega on one side and a blue arum lily on the other. On each side of the front window hung panels with dancing figures painted by Duncan Grant and Vanessa Bell. The two showrooms were on the ground floor divided by a large curtain of 'Adam and Eve' by Henri Doucet. Sometimes there would be an exhibition of paintings or drawings, at other times the rooms were filled with painted screens, tables, drapes of cloth and smaller items, and there was always a portfolio of current work for clients to inspect. The workrooms were on the floor above. The top floor was let.

The Omega sold an enormous range of items, from painted furniture to menu cards. The firm of J. Kallenborn and Sons produced their designs for marquetry tables, cupboards and trays; like most of Fry's suppliers, they were nearby, in Stanhope Street, off the Euston Road. The cupboards and tables which were specially made for decoration are recognizable by their attractive proportions, but were obviously cheaply produced. Elegant, tall-backed chairs with cane seats and backs were made to Roger's design by Dryad Ltd of Leicester, the wood generally painted red in imitation of lacquer and sometimes decorated with gold leaf. Prices ranged from £1 10s. for a painted table to £2 10s. for one of the cane chairs. (By comparison, Morris & Co. in Oxford Street were offering their rush-seated 'Sussex' armchair – introduced by William Morris in the 1860s to solve identical furnishing problems – for 9s. 9d., and a solid oak trestle table designed by Philip Webb cost £12 5s.) The Omega catalogue gave furnishing suggestions, such as a settee covered in black velvet for £12 12s. which would make 'an excellent background for brightly coloured cushions'. A service providing murals, stained glass (made by a firm in Fulham) and mosaics was offered. A casual shopper could purchase screens, boxes, lamps, trays, toys and bead necklaces, and also dresses, fans, parasols and opera bags.

Textiles, either hand-painted or designed by the Omega artists, were a vital part of the overall 'look' of the place. This was the field in which the Omega was most copied by other firms. Names for the half-dozen printed linens were supposedly given by the German Ambassador's wife, Princess Lichnowsky, at the opening party. They were 'White', 'Maud' (named after Lady Cunard), 'Mechtilde' (named after herself), 'Amenophis', 'Margery' and 'Pamela' (the last two named after Fry's sister and daughter). They were produced in a range of colours, all 31 in. (79 cm) wide, and variously priced from 2s. 9d. to 4s. per yard. They were designed by Fry, Grant and Etchells and printed in France by the firm Besselievre in Maromme. Vanessa designed 'Cracow', a Jacquard-woven furnishing tapestry made by Messrs A. H. Lee & Sons Ltd. It too came in various colours, was 54 in. (137 cm) wide and cost 15s. 6d. In a photograph of the drawing room at 7 Dalmeny Avenue in north London, where Roger moved in 1919, 'Cracow' can be seen on the settee, with Duncan Grant's 'Elephant' tray in the background. Henri Gaudier-Brzeska also designed a marquetry

A page from the Omega catalogue advertising jointed wooden toy animals.

Animals in jointed wood, hand-painted in the workshops, made from designs by our artists. The patent supports of the feet enable these animals to take innumerable dramatic poses.

The designs are made with a view to seizing the character of the animal rather than to literal imitation.

Omega moveable animals strongly made in three-ply wood:—

Camels	-	Large Size	**7/6**	...	Small Size **1/6**
Rhinoceros	,,	,,	**7/6**	...	,, ,, **1/6**
Elephants	,,	,,	**10/6**		
Tigers	,,	,,	**10/6**		
		Windmills	...	...	**3/-**

Omega Doll's-Houses and Puppet Stages.

tray called 'The Wrestlers' and Vanessa a completely abstract one, all made by Kallenborns.

Hand-dyed curtains, cushions, bedspreads, chair-covers, painted silk stoles and scarves and other items in silk or linen were also for sale, as were collage hangings and embroidered panels, which were generally designed by Grant and worked in needlepoint by Vanessa and by Mrs Miles, the caretaker's wife. The Omega sold batiks which were produced by a Manchester firm for sale abroad. Painted lampshades cost 4s. 6d. for silk, 2s. for card. Carpets were produced, both hand-knotted and loom woven. At first they were made in France, but later the commercial firm Wilton Royal, after first spurning the Omega designs, agreed to weave them for the Workshops. Painted tiles and pottery were also on sale.

Roger knew many of the fashionable London hostesses and obviously counted on their patronage in the hope that their example would spread the Omega's reputation. Lady Ottoline Morrell, Lady Cunard, Lady Drogheda and Lady Desborough were all customers. There were also many people connected with the world of arts and letters who visited and bought there, but their interest stemmed primarily from acquaintance or friendship with the people involved. Augustus John, Shaw, Arnold Bennett, E. M. Forster, G. L. Dickinson, Rupert Brooke, Ezra Pound, W. B. Yeats, the Sitwells, and Vanessa's sister, Virginia Woolf, were all familiar with the Omega. London intellectual circles, however, lacked the showmanship of the Paris *monde* where Poiret gave extravagant parties and where people enjoyed being linked with daring and modern enterprises. Roger was reluctant to advertise the Omega other than by word of mouth, with the result that it never became known as a regular business.

The Omega soon faced competition. A French journalist, X. Marcel Boulestin, who had been living in London for several years working as private secretary to the playwright and translator Cosmo Gordon Lennox, was a friend of Max Beerbohm and knew many of London's celebrities. In November 1913 he opened a showroom in his own flat in Elizabeth Street, Belgravia. He admired the bold colours of the Ballets Russes and the new French designers, such as André Groult and Paul Iribe (who in 1908 had produced the illustrated *Les Robes de Paul Poiret*). He sold their designs and work from Darmstadt, Munich and Vienna, as well as some African art. When Poiret visited London to supervise the costumes for Charles Cochran's ballet *Afgar* at the Pavilion Theatre, he visited Boulestin and agreed to let him sell the complete range of Martine wallpapers and fabrics. Boulestin's venture was apparently successful: in his autobiography he claimed that he started with £100 and in nine months had taken £3,000 in sales and private commissions for decoration. His clientèle included London's fashionable society, many of whom, such as Lady Curzon, Lady Drogheda, Syrie Maugham (then Mrs Wellcome) and Princess Lichnowsky, also patronized the Omega. Among the items sent to Boulestin's by the Martine was a low divan with silk, fur, gold and silver cushions, forerunner of the interior Poiret was to show at the Paris Salon d'Automne in 1919 with low divans suitable for 'smoking opium'. Such ideas probably amused Boulestin's wealthy customers more than Fry's earnest desire to popularize Post-Impressionism and would no doubt have scandalized him by their lack of serious artistic intent. Upon the outbreak of war, Boulestin returned to France. An attempt to revive his business in 1919 failed completely.

Roger had never shown any interest in mainstream European design. During the Arts and Crafts Movement, which had initially inspired the European workshops, most designers had been trained architects. Roger himself had been briefly involved with that movement when, after leaving Cambridge, he had worked for a time at Toynbee Hall in the East End of London with his friend C. R. Ashbee. Ashbee had gone on to found the Guild of Handicraft with the nucleus of his evening class from Toynbee Hall and was one of the most important followers of William Morris's ethic of craftsmanship. In 1895 Roger had executed a fresco of a formal landscape garden for the chimneybreast in the drawing room of Ashbee's Chelsea house, the Magpie and Stump. In the previous year he had also designed furniture for the Cambridge rooms of an old schoolfriend, John McTaggart.

Ashbee, whose socialist-influenced Guild failed financially in 1907, hated the productions of the Omega. Roger visited him in Chipping Campden in July 1913 and was evidently rather tedious, talking endlessly about 'his little group of Post-Impressionists'. Ashbee's friends considered the Omega

> TOO AWFUL, simply a *crime* against truth and beauty . . . *Berlin wool-work* mats and bags, ghastly cushions and curtains looking as if they had fallen by mistake into several dye vats – hot muddy and chalky colours, pink, acrid mauve, lemon and a sort of cocoa colour – I am sure you would loathe it all.[17]

The Omega Workshops have been described as a last outpost of the Arts and Crafts Movement, but this was never so. Roger rejected the kind of socialism which many of the English designers had espoused and never considered the Omega products in relation to architecture. His only interest was painting and his stress on design was connected solely with his aesthetic theories, never with design in a formal structural sense, as it was to be interpreted later by the Bauhaus or by Le Corbusier. He therefore remained uninterested in the developments in France, such as the burgeoning Art Deco style, or in the work of men such as Josef Hoffmann in Austria, Richard Riemerschmid in Germany or Gerrit Rietveld in Holland, although he emulated their recognition of the importance of co-operation between designers which had led to the establishment of several workshops.

For this reason it was impossible that the Omega should ever develop in any coherent stylistic direction. It had two aims, to promote English

Post-Impressionism and, as Quentin Bell later put it, to provide 'jobs for the boys'. The rationale behind the Workshops' productions was given by Roger in his preface to the Omega catalogue:

If you look at a pot or a woven cloth made by a negro savage of the Congo with the crude instruments at his disposal, you may begin by despising it for its want of finish. If you put them beside a piece of modern Sèvres china or a velvet brocade from a Lyons factory, you will perhaps begin by congratulating yourself upon the wonders of modern industrial civilization, and think with pity of the poor savage. But if you will allow the poor savage's handiwork a longer contemplation you will find something in it of greater value and significance than in the Sèvres china or Lyons velvet.

It will become apparent that the negro enjoyed making his pot or cloth, that he pondered delightedly over the possibilities of his craft and that his enjoyment finds expression in many ways; and as these become increasingly apparent to you, you share his joy in creation, and in that forget the roughness of the result. On the other hand the modern factory products were made almost entirely for gain, no other joy than that of money making entered into their creation. You may admire the skill which has been revealed in this, but it can communicate no disinterested delight.

The artist is the man who creates not only for need but for joy, and in the long run mankind will not be content without sharing that joy through the possession of real works of art, however humble or unpretentious they may be.

The Omega Workshops, Limited is a group of artists who are working with the object of allowing free play to the delight in creation in the making of objects for common life. They refuse to spoil the expressive quality of their work by sand-papering it down to a shop finish, in the belief that the public has at last seen through the humbug of the machine-made imitation of works of art. They endeavour to satisfy practical necessities in a workmanlike manner, but not to flatter by the pretentious elegance of the machine-made article. They try to keep the spontaneous freshness of primitive or peasant work while satisfying the needs and expressing the feelings of modern cultivated man.[18]

Roger never expected his artists to become involved in the structural design or making of the furniture, nor in the techniques of fabric printing or rug weaving. For a start, this would have been too time-consuming and craftsmanship had nothing to do with his aim of furthering Post-Impressionism. If clients came into the Omega showroom and looked through the portfolio of current designs for screens or cushions, or liked a fabric, then perhaps they could be persuaded to appreciate a framed canvas by the same artist. The public would, he hoped, gradually learn that the integrity and success of a design could be as valid on a pencil box as in a picture. Roger was not down-grading the importance of art: like William

Morris before him, he considered that the decorative arts could be useful in training the eye to appreciate beauty – in this case the beauty that he saw as created out of mass, colour and form.

The first major undertaking by the Omega after its opening in July 1913 was a commission to contribute a Post-Impressionist room to the Ideal Home Exhibition sponsored annually by the *Daily Mail*, to be held from 9 to 25 October at the Olympia Exhibition Hall in London. Considering the furore caused by Roger's Post-Impressionist Exhibition only three years earlier, this was an important step towards wider recognition of the new style. The Omega was to present a sitting room with hand-dyed cushions, printed curtains and upholstery on a 'general theme of designs based on the movements of the dance'.

From this first large commission sprang the Omega's first major problem. In October Wyndham Lewis, Cuthbert Hamilton, Edward Wadsworth and Frederick Etchells sent out a letter – known as the 'round robin' – to all the people associated with the Omega, claiming that the *Daily Mail* had in fact commissioned Wyndham Lewis and Spencer Gore to contribute the room and had asked the Omega merely to supply the furniture. They claimed that this request was the result of the *Daily Mail*'s admiration of the decorations carried out by Lewis, Gore and Charles Ginner in May 1912 at a Soho nightclub called The Cave of the Golden Calf. The 'round robin' asserted that Fry had wrongly taken the commission for himself and the Omega, hiding from Lewis the true nature of the request. A further accusation was that Fry had deliberately not passed on to Etchells a request from Leeds Art Gallery to contribute some paintings for an exhibition. Lewis also claimed that Fry had wilfully ignored him when undertaking the mural decoration for the room, asking him instead to carve a mantelpiece. The signatories summed up: 'More incidents of the above nature could be alleged, but these two can be taken as diagnostic of the general tone of the place.' A parting insult closed the letter:

> As to its tendencies in Art, they alone would be sufficient to make it very difficult for any vigorous art-instinct to long remain under that roof. The Idol is still Prettiness, with its mid-Victorian languish of the neck, and its skin is 'greenery-yallery', despite the Post-What-Not fashionableness of its draperies. This family party of strayed and Dissenting Aesthetes, however, were compelled to call in as much modern talent as they could find, to do the rough and masculine work without which they knew their efforts would not rise above the level of a pleasant tea-party, or command more attention.[19]

Lewis was in fact vindictively levelling the same criticisms at the Omega that Vanessa had voiced to Roger in 1912 when she feared that its output might be 'really sweet and too pretty and small' in conception. The Omega never really produced pretty items, although in the hands of some of the minor artists who worked there it did tend to become quaint and petty and Roger's insistence on design was narrowed down to mere patterning. In comparison with the works of Matisse or Picasso, the English painters did lack, not a boldness, but a grandeur of conception. They were modern, but seldom great.

The way in which Lewis left the Omega with this declaration was a preface to his future activities. In the same manner he had engineered a confrontation with Walter Sickert over the formation of the London Group. In April 1914 he published *Blast* No. 1 and went on to found his own 'Rebel Art Centre'. If he had meekly seceded from the Omega he could not have convincingly set himself up as a rebel nor, in the pages of *Blast*, vowed to 'destroy politeness, standardization and academic, that is, civilized, vision'. Lewis's tactics were those of invective, struggle, rebellion and performance and were based upon his theory of art: there was to be no romantic gazing at art, only passionate involvement with it deep in the vortex. In *Blast* No. 2 he attacked the Omega and, after the First World War, continued to blame the group he had left for, as he saw it, deliberately throttling his reputation as an artist.

So far as the Omega was concerned, the altercation was soon resolved. Roger was painting with Henri Doucet in France at the time, but Molly MacCarthy telephoned Vanessa at the Omega and told her of the 'round robin'. During the next few days Vanessa was in touch with the *Daily Mail* officials, all of whom confirmed that the commission had been given to the Omega and that the names of Gore and Lewis had not been mentioned. Roger was also vindicated over the Leeds episode. That such arguments were to Lewis the lifeblood of art and had little to do with personal antagonisms was borne out when Clive Bell ran into him soon after and Lewis claimed ingenuously that he had had little to do with the writing of the letter. Lewis, Wadsworth, Hamilton and Etchells never returned to the Omega. Vanessa wrote to Roger the day after the rumpus, saying that she had been to the Omega that morning to paint some lampshades and that 'Jessie and Winnie were there of course, no one else. Duncan is going to do a table tomorrow. It's very peaceful. I expect we shall soon get other artists to go on alright.'[20]

In retrospect it does not matter greatly that Vorticism developed independently of the Omega. Left without the inevitable machinations of Lewis, the Workshops continued to establish their own individual, if gentler, style, notably through the contributions of Duncan Grant and Vanessa. If the episode harmed the Omega in any way, it was by detracting from its publicity as an *enfant terrible* of the art world, a reputation that Lewis wanted for himself.

The life of the Omega went on. In December 1913 an exhibition of recent work was held at Fitzroy Square and a nursery and model bedroom shown. The nursery, with panels by Vanessa which she believed were 'a most truthful portrait of Indian and African animal life', and a ceiling painted by Winifred Gill, was complete with jointed wooden toys by Roger and a doll's house. (The decorations remained in the large upstairs room, and thenceforth the artists' workshop was called 'the nursery'.) In February 1914 textiles, furniture and pottery were shown at the Sandon Society in Liverpool in association with an exhibition of paintings bought by the Contemporary Art Society. In March Lady Hamilton commissioned Roger to decorate her home in Hyde Park Gardens. He contributed some stained glass, Vanessa a mosaic pavement for the entrance hall and Gaudier-Brzeska some stone pots. Three rooms in all were decorated and furnished. Some time early that year the Omega must have exhibited its products in Oxford. Pamela Diamand, Roger's daughter, remembers such a show and Raymond Mortimer, then a student at Oxford, bought some Omega curtain fabric.

In May the Omega exhibited 85 pieces at the Whitechapel Exhibition of Twentieth Century Art and in June it was included in the Allied Artists' Exhibition in Holland Park, as was Lewis's Rebel Art Centre. Gaudier-Brzeska reviewed the exhibition in *The Egoist* and gave his opinion of the Rebel Art Centre stand: 'A desire to employ the most vigorous forms of decorations fills it with fans, scarves, boxes and a table, which are the finest of those objects I have seen.'[21] At the Omega stand he admired the subtlety of a black and white carpet, marquetry tables and trays and the pottery, but was irritated by the 'prettiness' of the fabrics and hangings on show.

In November the Omega held its own show of paintings and works. During the first year Roger obviously worked hard to include the Omega in as many outside exhibitions as possible in order to publicize the new business. The Whitechapel exhibition, for example, where the Omega showed a complete range of items from parasols to cartoons for mosaics, attracted over 53,000 visitors in six weeks. His unceasing energy consolidated the firm as a viable financial concern and it had begun to show a slight profit. After his return from France following the Ideal Home walk-out he had written to his mother:

> It certainly arouses an immense amount of interest, but also bitter opposition. I suppose it's natural that people should dislike it when you try to do something new, but I'm always a little surprised at the vehemence and the personal antagonism that it stirs up. Oddly enough, the people from whom I get most intelligent sympathy are our competitors in the trade.[22]

Roger certainly had a fund of ready and willing support among his young artists, especially the women artists from the Slade who were only too anxious to find a place in what was still very much a man's world, even if what they did, as Barbara Bagenal remembers, was mostly hanging pictures and helping with customers. And of course Roger was delighted to share his enthusiasm with Vanessa.

Most of the artists were applying themselves to new techniques for the first time. In 1912 Vanessa had written to Clive that she was painting Quentin in his bath: 'It's rather fun painting again after doing all these patterns. Duncan has been trying to do a pattern but gets even more muddled than I do, in fact I don't think he'll ever master repeats.'[23] The Omega textiles are evidence that both Duncan and Vanessa did eventually master the technique. Edward Wolfe, a South African and the last artist to join the Omega, after being introduced to Roger by Nina Hamnett around 1917, recalls that the Omega was an extremely colourful and creatively exciting place, with an atmosphere that encouraged the artist to pick up and decorate whatever came to hand. The keynote of the Workshops was spontaneity. The artists could relax after their more serious painting and experiment with any ideas they had for decorative schemes.

One area where they were all forced to learn as they went along was ceramics. Roger first found a potter in Mitcham, Surrey, to throw pots for them to decorate, but he soon became dissatisfied with the set shapes that were all the man knew how to throw and decided to try throwing for himself. In the autumn of 1914 he went down to Poole in Dorset where he was able to experiment at Carter & Co.'s facilities after Winifred Gill had introduced him to the Carter family. Duncan and Vanessa also tried their hands, but it was Roger who persevered, while the others continued to decorate fired pieces. Roger made a prototype dinner service, plates, vases and tea and coffee sets from which moulds were produced so that further sets could be run off without his assistance. Tiles were also made and then painted. In the Omega catalogue Roger described pottery as 'essentially a form of sculpture' and he insisted that the sets made from his moulds should preserve all the surface irregularities of his originals, keeping the sensitivity of the working of the material. He used plain glazes, especially a white tin glaze, but also dark blue and black, and occasionally other colours as well. He was influenced in his choice by his knowledge of Chinese and Persian ceramics, although he admitted, when a turquoise glaze was admired by an expert from the British Museum, that its beauty had been achieved more by accident than by design.

In comparison with the ever more specialized approach of contemporary potters, such as W. Howson Taylor at the Ruskin Pottery or the designers working for Pilkington, with their insistence on glaze and decoration, Fry's conception of pottery was revolutionary for its time. One of the most popular designers then was Frank Brangwyn, who was associated with Royal Doulton, and who had previously worked for Morris & Co., for Samuel Bing in Paris and for Louis Comfort Tiffany in New York. His ceramics were a somewhat whimsical legacy of the Arts and Crafts Movement. In total contrast, Roger exploited his familiarity with much earlier ceramics, eschewing perfection of glaze and finish in favour of forms which were expressive of hands shaping and moulding the clay with all the necessary limitations of human fingers. Quentin Bell, himself a potter, described some Omega pottery for radio listeners in 1964, on the occasion of an exhibition of Omega products at the Victoria and Albert Museum:

> Look, for instance, at his white sauceboat. It is heavy, but admirably simple and yet without the over-conscious, aseptic simplicity of so much modern pottery. It consists of a series of rotund curves. The lip is almost a small hemisphere growing from a large hemisphere which is the bowl. The handle is a quarter of a circle which suddenly straightens out to join the bowl . . . I am afraid that this gives little idea of the amazingly strong and purposeful look of the thing. It is a prototype of the ceramics of our century. From it a generation has learned to avoid fussiness and indecision and yet it also has a sensual quality; the semi-opaque tin glaze is perfectly suited to the form and just discovers the gentle warmth of the earthenware body beneath. It is a useful reminder that simplicity need not be dull.[24]

At the end of 1914 the Omega received three decorative commissions in London. The first two, which Roger undertook with Duncan Grant and Vanessa, were for Henry Harris's house at 17 Bedford Square, Bloomsbury, and for Ethel Sands' dining room at 15 The Vale, Chelsea. The third was for the Cadena Café in Westbourne Grove, where not only rugs, tables, vases, lampshades and murals, but even the waitresses' clothes, were designed by the Omega. It is interesting to compare the overall impression of the Cadena Café with Charles Rennie Mackintosh's designs for the Willow Tea-rooms, which had opened in Glasgow in October 1904. The Cadena Café reveals the emphasis of the artist, while the Willow Tea-rooms show the concerns of the architect-designer. Both schemes have an overall integrity and coherence, but Mackintosh achieved this by a spatial use of decorative elements in the juxtaposition of horizontal and vertical features, which were picked up structurally in the staircase and wrought-iron balustrades as well as decoratively in the rugs and chairs. The Cadena Café showed little concern for the three-dimensional occupation of the space, relying on a coherence of flat, painterly surfaces in murals and fabrics. It is this insistence on decoration rather than structural design, and the acceptance of existing space, which characterized the Omega. The reliance on decoration was utilized to full advantage and pinpoints the essential improvization which was the basis of the Omega style. Given a wall, a table, a screen, a box, the artists felt free to cover it as they wished.

The freedom of surface application, the assumption that anything could present a valid opportunity to exercise the imagination, was echoed in the artists' choice of subject-matter. What had originally shocked people in Post-Impressionist painting was as much the choice of the images as the unfamiliar use of line, mass and colour. Casual observations, flicks of the wrist, as it were, suddenly became legitimate images through which to present an artistic statement. Raymond Mortimer wrote of Duncan Grant's work at this time:

> He began a series of paintings that are without a parallel in the history of the British School. A bunch of flowers, a woman in a bath-rub, a lamp on a table, a coster with a greyhound, a group of ballet-dancers, a friend sitting in a garden – anything, indeed, that caught his eye and memory provided a theme upon which he would elaborate a fantasia.[25]

In 1918 Roger wrote to Vanessa describing his appreciation of Duncan's artistic vision:

I think I'd felt, going about London with Duncan, more than ever how wonderful his visual life is, how infinitely quick he is in his reaction to sight, how he misses the point of nothing. He can look at every face in the street and never miss one that has something in it, and all the time be seeing the whole effect and all with such curious imaginative intensity.

I think his Hat Shop is wonderful and is typical of what's best and most characteristic in him. It's what I've always said; the element of the object with all its ordinary associations comes in ... There's a point not exactly of wit but of delicate and half-humorous fantasy about it. It's splendid as coherence of form, but that's not at all the point. He ought to flâneur [*sic*] in London or Paris for at least two hours every day. He ought never to shut himself up in the country. [Duncan Grant was not then in London but living at Charleston in Sussex with Vanessa Bell.] He ought always to watch for a subject in the very modified sense in which I've used it: the fact being that only some such 'subject', a thing with a delicate point that one could almost (never quite) put into words, only such a subject inspires him to the best of his purely formal sensibility.[26]

For Roger, Duncan represented a continuation of all he admired in the contemporary French painters. The 'fantasy' of Duncan's imaginative life was eminently suited to the decoration of screens and panels and even to smaller items such as fans and boxes. It is Duncan's imagination that dominates the best work of the Omega.

The lightness of touch shown in the choice of both subject-matter and surface was echoed by a light-heartedness about what was made. It was important to be creative, but the casualness with which the rest of the process of production was treated led to the frequent criticism of the Omega for selling objects which were not well made and often fell to bits. Madge Vaughan, a friend of Virginia Woolf's, bought a lampshade, some fabrics and a long painted bench, decorated by Roger, at the Omega in October 1913. Vanessa reported to Roger that 'she liked quite a lot of the things but thought many too expensive especially the necklaces'.[27] Madge paid £5 for the bench, and the following spring Vanessa was telling Roger: 'Madge said that the seat she bought has been much admired but being out of doors in the frost, all the paint has come off! I said I thought we could probably send her a pot of the right colour with directions how to paint it again.'[28] Such a casual attitude was consistent with the artists' views on their activities, and perhaps even endearing to friends who appreciated and wished to support their endeavours. The Omega was ultimately an artists' workshop rather than a shop. But the stance may well have seemed precious to ordinary customers, who bought once because they liked what they saw but would be unlikely to buy a second time. However, the enduring joke about the fast rate of decomposition of Omega objects stemmed from the exception rather than the rule, and has been rather overplayed.

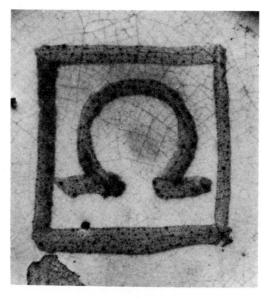

The Omega mark used on ceramics. This is the painted version; another was impressed.

XII *'Vases' carpet designed by Duncan Grant and woven by Wilton Royal for Virginia Woolf in 1932.*

XIII   Cotton fabric designed by Vanessa Bell for Allan Walton, 1933–34.

XIV   Duncan Grant's bedroom at Charleston. The door and fireplace were
decorated by Vanessa Bell in 1916, the painted linen chest by Duncan Grant in 1916
or 1917, and the embroidered music stool by Duncan Grant in 1925 (see ill. 35); the
rug is by Douglas Davidson.

XV   The dining room at Charleston, decorated in the 1930s. The painted table is by ▷
Vanessa Bell, the chairs from the Omega, and the ceramic lamp by Quentin Bell.

XVI   Bedroom cupboard at Charleston decorated by Duncan Grant c.1930.

◁XVII   Door painted by Duncan Grant in what used to be Clive Bell's study at Charleston and is now the kitchen. The upper panel was painted in 1917; the original subject of the lower panel was repainted in 1961.

XVIII   *The drawing room at Charleston, decorated in
the 1930s: the walls were stencilled and painted by
Vanessa Bell, the overmantel painted (and later altered)
by Duncan Grant.*

◁ XIX   Duncan Grant's studio at Charleston in 1977. The screen on the left was
painted by Duncan for the Omega opening in 1913 (see pl. II). Above the fireplace –
decorated by Duncan – is a photograph of Vanessa Bell, and on the table at the left is
a flower-study which Duncan was working on at the time.

XX   The pulpit at Berwick Church, painted by Duncan Grant after vandals had
destroyed the original by Vanessa Bell in 1962.

2

Vanessa Bell and the development of an idea

DURING the time when Roger Fry was busy arranging exhibitions, finding premises for the Omega and contacting manufacturers, his love affair with Vanessa Bell was slowly unfolding.

At the age of sixteen Vanessa, the eldest of Leslie Stephen's children by Julia Duckworth, lost her mother. Two years later her stepsister Stella died, and she became head of the family. Leslie Stephen was ill, obsessive and difficult, and her sister Virginia had already manifested mental instability. Vanessa possessed a strength which others were quick to rely upon, confident that she could cope easily with the responsibility both for them and for herself.

After their father's death in 1904 the Stephens – Vanessa, Virginia, Thoby and Adrian – settled together at No. 46 Gordon Square, where they established their own relatively unrestricted way of life, and where they were visited frequently by Thoby's Cambridge friends. In 1906 their adored brother Thoby died of typhoid, contracted during a family holiday in Greece and Turkey. Less than three months later Vanessa married Thoby's friend, Clive Bell. She had previously refused his offers of marriage, saying that while she appreciated his friendship, she was not in love with him. However, she accepted his third proposal, made two days after Thoby's death.

Another Cambridge friend, Lytton Strachey, described Clive in 1905:

His character has several layers, but it is difficult to say which is the fond. There is the country gentleman layer which makes him retire into the depths of Wiltshire to shoot partridges. There is the Paris decadent layer, which takes him to the quartier latin where he discusses painting and vice with American artists and French models. There is the eighteenth-century layer which adores Thoby Stephen. There is the layer of innocence which adores Thoby's sister. There is the layer of prostitution, which shows itself in an amazing head of crimped straw-coloured hair. And there is the layer of stupidity which runs transversely through all the other layers.[1]

Clive was undoubtedly proud of his beautiful wife for her poise, her emancipation, and her ability to be on equal terms with his friends, whom she had met through Thoby. But he probably regarded her painting as secondary to her place as his wife and companion and did not become involved, as Roger later did, in her pressing day-to-day absorptions with brushes, paint and canvas. It was not until Roger entered her life that her letters to Clive became full of what she was painting.

After their marriage, the Bells remained in the Gordon Square house while Virginia moved with Adrian to nearby Fitzroy Square. With a child soon on the way, Vanessa was happy and secure. Virginia constantly referred to Vanessa as a rich and fecund figure, full of wisdom and hospitality for those who lacked her own private pivotal centre of family life. In September, when Vanessa was five months pregnant and staying with her sister in Sussex, Virginia wrote of her to a friend: 'Nessa is here, and we talk – when her husband is gone for a walk alone and that is seldom – of art and life, and marriage and motherhood, and she always comes back to it – being the richest and ripest old creature under the sun – that Art is the only thing; the lasting thing, though the others are splendid.'[2]

During the spring following Julian's birth Vanessa's happiness in her marriage was shaken when Virginia and Clive entered into a flirtation, encouraged by common resentment of Vanessa's attention to the baby. In June 1910 Virginia had another minor breakdown when Vanessa was seven months pregnant with her second child, Quentin. After his birth Quentin failed to gain weight; Clive did not share her anxiety, and Vanessa found that there was no one in whom she could confide.

Roger had gradually begun visiting Gordon Square more regularly and Vanessa admired him for his wide knowledge of art and of the dealers' world, although she still regarded him as one of the older, prestigious members of the New English Art Club. (He was thirteen years her senior.) However, she soon found a more personal link with him when he discovered her anxiety over the baby's health. Having two young children of his own, he could readily sympathize with her. For the first time Vanessa had someone who shared her two foremost concerns, painting and her children.

During the tour of Turkey in the spring of 1911 Vanessa discovered the joy of travelling with Roger, who was experienced and enthusiastic and knew how to enter into the indigenous life of a country rather than remaining, in Edwardian fashion, on the polite outskirts of the established tourist routes. This was perfect for them as painters, as he wrote to his wife from Brusa:

> Vanessa and I managed to do a sketch this morning of the Turkish cemetery with cypresses in front of a great mountain slope. We sat just outside a weaver's house – he was a dear old man who beamed on us and then brought out Turkish coffee for us and invited us to come and sit in his garden, where there was a little stream bubbling up in a tiny marble basin.[3]

This pleasure was cut short by Vanessa's fainting fits and her eventual miscarriage. She did not recover quickly and for a long time after her return to England she was unwell with neuralgia and nervous problems. She continued to have fainting fits and often suffered a curious and unpleasant withdrawal from her surroundings. At first her doctors advised her to get back to normal life, but this had little effect on her condition. Roger then arranged for her to see a nerve specialist, who advised a long and careful recuperation. He spent as much time with her as he could and in July she wrote appreciatively to him, saying that 'being with you is like being on a river and being with most people is like driving a jibbing horse along a bumpy road'.[4]

That summer of 1911, while Vanessa slowly recuperated, was long and hot. She went first to stay with Virginia in Sussex, and then with Clive and the children to her parents-in-law in Wiltshire. She had little in common with them at the best of times, and their affluent lifestyle now exacerbated her nervous state. Clive's family had no interest in art and she even found the countryside uninteresting to paint. Her illness gave her the excuse to keep to herself, her only escape being in long letters to Roger. He was himself a prolific letter writer in the tradition of large Victorian families, and their letters show a frankness and humour that bespeak both trust and a thorough knowledge of one another.

When the Bells left Wiltshire, Vanessa persuaded Clive to take a house in Guildford where she could be near to Roger's home, Durbins. Millmead Cottage had a garden running down to the Thames and there Vanessa could sit and do a little sketching, for she had been unable to paint for some time due to her illness. Roger was busy in London with the Borough Polytechnic murals, but he often visited, bringing with him Duncan Grant who was working with him on a mosaic of badminton players in the summer house at Durbins. They would swim in the river or sketch Vanessa, who had little excuse for not sitting still. Late in September

Vanessa and her children went to Studland Bay in Dorset, where she had spent several previous holidays, and Roger took a house nearby with his sister Joan and his children, Julian and Pamela. The demands of the children cut down the amount of time they could spend together, and besides, Clive was beginning to be jealous of Roger's attention to Vanessa; so the holiday was not entirely a success. In January, however, Roger and Vanessa took a house together in Springvale in the Isle of Wight. Vanessa had now recovered her health, and they were able to do a lot of painting and were extremely happy.

By this time Clive had probably been made aware of their relationship. While Vanessa was ill, he had been resentful of Roger's more soothing presence. Clive himself had been of little help and his jealousy of Roger only increased Vanessa's nervousness. However, the Bells' marriage gradually became a relationship of mutual independence and fondness, and continued as a close friendship all their lives. In any case, Clive was seldom without a love affair of his own. He liked and admired Roger and based much of his own art criticism on Roger's theories (a fact that later often justifiably enraged Roger).

The people around Vanessa were gradually becoming more secure. Virginia and Adrian had moved to Brunswick Square, where they were joined by Duncan Grant, Maynard Keynes and, on his return from Ceylon, Leonard Woolf. In May came the welcome news of Virginia's engagement to Leonard; the couple were married the following August. Also, in February Virginia and Vanessa jointly took the lease on Asheham House in Sussex, which gave them both a place of their own where they could get away from London. Vanessa spent August and September at Asheham, preparing her work for the Second Post-Impressionist Exhibition, helping to design a poster advertising it and making curtains for the house. She had Julian and Quentin with her, and both Roger and Duncan Grant stayed there periodically.

Virginia once wrote to Vanessa,

> As a painter, I believe you are much less conscious of the drone of daily life than I am, as a writer. You *are* a painter. I think a good deal about you, for purposes of my own, and this seems to me clear. This explains your simplicity. What have you to do with all this turmoil? What you want is a studio where you can see things.[5]

It was Roger who really encouraged her to be a professional painter, and over the next few years she began to assert herself against all the demands upon her time, so that she was left with what was most important to her.

During the period from 1910 to 1913 Vanessa painted some of her best and most distinctive work, characterized by the delineation of shape and mass, organized to form a deliberate design. Although some of her portraits at this time, such as those of Virginia, make no attempt to show features or details, friends said that they could always unmistakably recognize the sitter. Vanessa's paintings were highly individual, both in the solidity of the design and in the use of colour. Her best paintings are of her friends and her children, showing an intensity of vision of the familiar events and surroundings in her life. Unlike Duncan Grant, she seldom attempted to form a design from an abstraction of something seen, and the apparent domesticity of some of her subjects intensifies the power of her interpretation. Her vision is feminine, her subjects belonging to the world of women – Julian in his pram or 'nursery tea'. Her paintings owe their effect to the heightened reality of the artist's view rather than to the choice of a less familiar but more objectively exciting subject.

Two elements of life were always of the greatest importance to her, travel and her children. In May 1912 a visit to Italy with Clive and Roger revitalized her visual ideas, as she wrote to Roger from London on her return:

> England looked too dreary for words. I tried not to look but kept catching myself trying to see the people in the country, expecting to find nice colours or something as one does with every peasant in Italy. But all was drab and hideous.[6]

> Oh God I wish I were in France too painting those colours. London is too awful. I can see nothing out of doors. It's all so dingy. I get stared at in my blue Florentine hat almost as much as I did at Pisa. I can only suppose because everyone else is in brown or grey. Quentin is the one spot of satisfactory colour with his orange hair in a bright pink dress. I am already hoping to go abroad again.[7]

The company of the children at Asheham was a constant source of pleasure and she regaled Clive with accounts of their exploits as she taught Julian to read or observed Quentin trying to beat the wind away with his hands. She had a remarkable talent for seeing things from their level: this in turn added a richness to her own perceptions.

Vanessa's sense of design came from her increasing familiarity with the French Post-Impressionists and reflected Roger's critical concerns. The group of artists who came together after the initial Post-Impressionist exhibition at the Grafton began not only to talk but to paint together. Roger wrote to McKnight Kauffer at a later date: 'The whole question of groups and competition is very difficult. Art generally seems to flourish only where there are enough people interested in the same kind of thing to create a kind of spiritual high-tension . . .'8 This meant that a certain colony mentality was required, the forming of a crucible from which new and distinctively modern statements would emerge. This was what Roger hoped for above all from both the Grafton Group and the Omega.

At this time Vanessa gave Roger the kind of support and inspiration which he needed for his own painting and a feeling of equilibrium which helped him in sustaining his plans for the future. He wrote,

> Oh Nessa, it was good, our little married life, and no one but you could have brought it off. I look at the drawings which malign you so but still do remind me of the sight of you on the black sofa. Nessa, I should be a real artist, really truly and without doubt if I could draw you often, because you have this miracle of rhythm in you, and not in your body only, but in everything you do. It all has the same delightful reasonableness, and, after all beauty is a kind of reasonableness, you know. It means ease in all the things round you and in all your relations . . .9

Roger was a tall man, although photographs of him and people's descriptions somehow suggest that he was slight; possibly his intense energy and vitality give the impression of his being bottled up in a small space. Vanessa, by contrast, appeared calm and resolute, sitting still before her easel, the mother figure in repose. Fry adored this aspect of her.

> I imagine all your gestures and how you'll be saying things and how all round you people will dare to be themselves and talk of anything and everything and no idea of shame or fear will come to them because you're there and they know you'll understand. And then I think of how beautifully you'll be walking about the rooms and how you'll take Quentin onto your knee and how patient you are and yet how you are just being yourself all the time and not making any huge effort just living very intensely and naturally and how perfectly reasonable you are (except when one meddles with your pictures) and yet how your being so reasonable is never dull or monotonous or too much expected and is in fact much more exciting to me than if you were all whims and caprices like the professionally seductive.10

Vanessa's confidence grew not only from Roger's emotional support but also from his practical help. Apart from her Friday Club shows, she had rarely exhibited her work and until 1912 had shown only one canvas a year with either the Allied Artists' Association or the New English Art Club. Roger now included six of her paintings at the Galerie Barbazanges exhibition in Paris and four in the Second Post-Impressionist Exhibition at the Grafton Galleries. In August 1912 she sold a painting for the first time, when the Contemporary Art Society bought *The Spanish Model* for five guineas; she was obviously delighted.

Another person who now increasingly began to add to Vanessa's visual experience was Duncan Grant, with whom she spent more and more time painting. He was six years younger than she; Vanessa had known him for several years, as he was a cousin of Thoby's Cambridge friend Lytton Strachey. The Strachey and Stephen families had been acquainted for two generations and Duncan had lived with his aunt, Lady Strachey, during his schooldays. In 1908, when he spent Christmas Eve with Virginia and Adrian, Virginia described him to Clive as 'difficult, but charming'; he had 'too many ideas, and no way of getting rid of them'. In 1910 a sketch by Duncan was given the place of honour at Vanessa's Friday Club exhibition, and Vanessa called him 'the most interesting of the young painters'. During 1912 their work was increasingly compared. In September, when Vanessa was at Asheham preparing for the Grafton show, she wrote to Roger:

> I find that I am not much improved by working with Duncan although of course I always think why didn't I see it like that? But as I have come to the conclusion that I didn't see it like that I no longer try to think I did – I suppose one would get used to working with anyone in time.[11]

By the end of that year they were good friends. At Christmas, Vanessa stayed alone in London while Clive took the children to his parents; she was unwell and Duncan came to visit her:

> I was interrupted yesterday by Duncan who came in and lay on the floor and talked in a desultory but cheering way of . . . how we are to turn my studio into a tropical forest with great red figures on the walls – a blue ceiling with birds of paradise floating from it (my idea) and curtains each one different. This is all to cheer us through London winters. Duncan also wants a bath let into the floor but I told him that was à la Leighton House which made him rather cross.[12]

In the spring of 1913 Duncan accompanied Roger and the Bells to Italy, returning via Paris. They bought crockery and fabrics in Ravenna to sell at the Omega but at Urbino there were disagreements between Roger and Clive, who wanted to sightsee, and Vanessa and Duncan, who preferred to settle somewhere and take life more easily. It was during this time that Vanessa first began to assert her independence from Roger. When his enthusiasm led him to set the pace and expect others to follow she quietly withdrew.

On their return the Omega opened and, as Vanessa later wrote to Roger, 'I think that in a way that did change things a good deal. It meant that I saw much more of you in a very exasperating way.'[13] Gradually she came to feel that while Roger wanted 'the kind of secret understanding between us that can only come when two people are in love with each other', she was no longer able to support that kind of private commitment. She was now painting more than ever; Julian and Quentin were at the time-consuming ages of five and three; she had two households to manage – Gordon Square and Asheham; and in the autumn she faced the demands of supervising Virginia's recovery from a suicide attempt. Vanessa always depended on a special fundamental sympathy with Roger but her gradual withdrawal from him was a defensive reaction against the claims he made on her. It is worth remembering Leonard Woolf's comment that her apparent tranquillity was superficial, that 'in the depths there was also an extreme sensitivity, a nervous tension which had some resemblance to the mental instability of Virginia'.

Vanessa had married Clive at a time when she desperately needed stability. Her relationship with Roger also began when she was anxious for her children and her marriage and required encouragement in her work. It was as though she had used these two men at times of crisis, only to shrug them off when, with their support, her troubles had been overcome. More likely she found that, in order to return love, she had to sacrifice the independence which, after the responsibilities she had had in her teens, was vital to her emotional security. Roger complained bitterly of her attitude towards him and she replied that his demands made it impossible for her to respond to him at all. Roger, however, despite his intense disappointment, refused to abandon their friendship altogether: 'I don't mean to let you push me over the line from which I couldn't come back.'[14]

Their affair ended in 1914. Although Vanessa then spent more and more time with Duncan, she did not leave Roger for him in the usual sexual implication of such a statement; Duncan, after all, was homosexual. Roger had given her the necessary encouragement to establish a way of life that would allow her to concentrate on her work. But, despite his own pleasure in painting, his life was too hectic for her and she did not share in his boundless intellectual interests. Ironically, in refusing Roger's entreaties, she was following his advice.

During the summer of 1913 Vanessa, Roger and Duncan had joined a group of friends camping at Brandon in Norfolk, which Vanessa described as an 'amazing fresh air cure'; she returned as brown as mahogany. On the train to Brandon Vanessa had 'found Duncan in his usual paint covered clothes but with a spotless new white hat, with about 20 packages, easel all coming to pieces, camp-stool, etc. and a bottle of champagne!'[15]

Duncan's second-hand clothes were a familiar joke. Vanessa, back in London, wrote to Clive in Scotland: 'Duncan who had meant to leave on Tuesday eventually failed to be ready in time to catch my train on Friday. However, as I had told him the next train was at 5.30 and it was really at 6 he did catch that and had been round here today to borrow 6/- and some paint.'[16] Beset by responsibilities and the need to answer Roger's demands, Vanessa was beginning to respond to Duncan's peculiar charm.

Duncan was universally loved and declared handsome, with a somewhat wistful and diffident style. His cousin, Lytton Strachey, had fallen in love with him in 1905 and in 1908 Duncan and Maynard Keynes became lovers. Duncan was generally short of money, but this was taken as an indulgent joke by those who lent him enough to tide him over. He never demanded, but was content to accept the help that friends offered: Lytton had consulted his brother-in-law Simon Bussy about Duncan's future, with the result that he went to study painting in Paris. Maynard had organized rooms in London and holidays in Greece, Turkey, Sicily, Tunis and Italy and continued to help and advise him. The reaction of Duncan's contemporaries to his memory is invariably a smile and a compliment.

Vanessa admired Duncan's casual attitude to life. His carefree behaviour created ease rather than a sense of pressure and was an antidote to her inherent seriousness. She wanted to be free to paint and here was a companion who not only shared her involvement with art but also set an example of how best to achieve the emotional independence she required. She could use her organizational abilities on his behalf without feeling weighed down. Vanessa's emotional needs were met by their closeness as painters, but Duncan never made her feel hemmed in by their friendship. In 1919 Virginia wrote perceptively of him to Vanessa:

I never saw a more remarkable figure than that adorable man – dressed in a non-conformist minister's coat; but under that an astonishing mixture of red waistcoats and jerseys, all so loose that they had to be hitched together by a woollen belt, and braces looping down somewhere quite useless. He is more and more like a white owl perched upon a branch and blinking at the light, and shuffling his soft furry feet in the snow – a wonderful creature, you must admit, though how he ever gets through life – but as a matter of fact he gets through it better than any of us.[17]

In May 1914 Vanessa accompanied Duncan to Paris for the opening of Jacques Copeau's production of *Twelfth Night* at the Théâtre du Vieux Colombier, for which Duncan had designed the costumes. As he hated the details of dressmaking, Vanessa had been helping him. The play received good reviews and the costumes were especially praised. In September they were painting together at Asheham and Vanessa wrote cheerily to Roger of their activities:

It is fine today and we have nailed up your canvas outside the house in front and have started on it. Duncan and I are each doing one. Do you mind? Perhaps I oughtn't to be, but it's such fun and if you don't like mine I will get more canvas for another! As a matter of fact I think unless I do one Duncan will never do his. We are doing two modern dress dancing figures in each – red, black, white, cadmium yellow and a little green – trying to keep them rather light and full of accent as I think with London greyness all round that's necessary.[18]

In October Duncan left his rooms in Brunswick Square and moved into the Bells' Gordon Square house, taking a studio in nearby Fitzroy Street.

Roger had hoped for some kind of artistic cooperative to result from the Omega, but in fact it brought Vanessa and Duncan closer together, leaving the other artists, including Roger, to work on their own. Roger's plans to work side by side with Vanessa on decorative commissions had to give way. At the beginning of 1915 he wrote to her:

. . . Look – you work with him constantly, you're his usual and constant pal, you play with him, you can spend a week in the country alone with him. He gives you everything except love and I'm pushed away into any place and only wanted when there's nothing better on . . .[19]

And in May he wrote to Clive:

You know I think you and Nessa have managed to make the only breathable atmosphere in England, at least for me. I can't quite put up with any other – only I feel a good deal less in the centre of things than I did . . .[20]

The end of his affair with Vanessa hurt Roger greatly and, combined with the desertion of Lewis and Etchells over the 'round robin', took away much of the lustre of his feelings about the Omega. The 'spiritual high-tension' was gone and the artists with whom he was left to work at the Omega could never rekindle his original enthusiasm. Within two years the impetus of his 'little group of Post-Impressionists' had petered out.

Design on the cover of 'Woodcuts by Various Artists', produced by the Omega in 1918.

3

The war years

TOWARDS the end of 1914 the Omega Workshops were beginning to feel the effects of the war, as it became obvious that the troops were not going to be 'home by Christmas'. Vanessa's circle of friends were all united against the war and the slaughter, but found themselves powerless and voiceless against the official machine and the overwhelming tide of public opinion. For many reasons, 1915 was not an easy year. Virginia had another serious mental breakdown in February. On 5 March Henri Doucet, Roger's painter friend who had worked at the Omega, was killed in action at the Front. Virginia's friend Rupert Brooke died at Skyros in the Dardanelles in April and on 5 June Henri Gaudier-Brzeska, who had at first refused to return to France to fight, was killed in the trenches. Duncan's cousin-in-law Simon Bussy, also a painter, enlisted in May and Nina Hamnett's Norwegian husband Roald Kristian was given three months' hard labour for failing to register as an alien and was deported to France in 1916.

In the autumn of 1914 Vanessa had written to Roger: 'Oh dear, it seems a gloomy enough world at present. One thinks that even the sort of thing one vaguely hoped for the children may be spoiled. However, it's no good – one must simply work and try and find out what is permanent.'[1]

Work continued at the Omega. In a time of prosperity and leisure the new ideas might gradually have taken root and developed into a distinctively modern style, seriously challenging the continuing popularity of Arts and Crafts designers such as C. F. A. Voysey or Ernest Gimson, but Post-Impressionism had completely dropped out of the news and the Workshops hardly had the chance to flourish.

In January 1915 Duncan made three jointed cardboard marionettes for a performance of Racine's *Bérénice*. They were 8 ft (2.4 m) high and D. H. Lawrence described them as 'titanic'. Also in January Roald Kristian made some African-looking marionettes which danced to Debussy's *Boîte à*

Joujoux at the Omega. There was a preview of Duncan's figures at a party Vanessa gave and a proper performance was held at the Omega the following month.

In April the Bells, Duncan and a new friend, David Garnett, a twenty-three-year-old student of botany whom they called Bunny, went to stay at Mary and St John Hutchinson's house, Eleanor, in Sussex. (Clive had recently begun an affair with Mary Hutchinson.) Vanessa spent some of her time at Eleanor making a dress for Marjorie Strachey; Lady Ottoline Morrell heard about it through Duncan and sent a message to say that she would like one too. This gave Vanessa the idea of making dresses for the Omega and interesting other friends, such as Iris Tree or Marie Beerbohm, in buying them. She wrote to sound out Roger: 'they could have a sort of dress parade, perhaps in Ottoline's drawing room and have a party to see them. If this could be done at the beginning of the season I believe it might be a great success.'[2] Roger approved the scheme; like Clive, he had, after all, often been the recipient of letters from Vanessa containing sketches and descriptions of her new dresses and coats, and had enjoyed buying local scarves and brightly coloured fabrics in the markets in Turkey when the three of them were there in 1911. He had already made a kind of shirt, brightly painted, which Nina Hamnett wore one evening at the fashionable Paris café, the Closerie des Lilas:

> I wore a jumper made on the same pattern as those Henri [Gaudier-Brzeska] and I wore in London, only it was of a large cubist design in blue, orange, and black. No one in Paris had seen anything quite like it and although Sonia Delaunay was already designing scarves, this was more startling. It was made and designed for the Omega Workshops by Roger Fry.[3]

Plans went ahead and various dressmakers were considered, including a Miss Kate Lechmere and Joy Brown, who had been governess to Fry's daughter at Durbins. Vanessa wrote to Roger in May that Miss Joy, as she was known, was 'much more in sympathy with us about colours and very anxious to carry out my ideas about cut'.[4] Vanessa had also been painting parasols and on 10 June an exhibition opened at the Omega with at least five dresses, several coats and waistcoats, evening cloaks, parasols and printed and dyed fabrics. Vanessa was pleased with the results and an arrangement was made with Douglas Pepler, who ran the Hampshire House Workshops which created work for Belgian refugees. Miss Joy was to work for him for £100 per year and to have the afternoons free to make dresses for the Omega on commission: the Omega would pay Mr Pepler

his usual rate per dress, and Miss Joy would also get 5 per cent. of the
Omega's profits on each dress. In that way the Omega avoided costly
overheads and paid only for specific commissions. This complicated
arrangement, however, did not ensure the success of the scheme: not
everyone liked Vanessa's dress designs or had the flair, like Ottoline
Morrell, to wear her choice of colour. Virginia remonstrated with her
when their sister-in-law, Karin Stephen, took to wearing Omega outfits:

> My God! What colours you are responsible for! Karin's clothes almost
> wrenched my eyes from the sockets – a skirt barred with reds and yellows of
> the vilest kind, and a pea green blouse on top, with a gaudy handkerchief on
> her head, supposed to be the very boldest taste. I shall retire into dove colour
> and old lavender, with a lace collar, and lawn wristlets.[5]

In July Vanessa and Winifred Gill were making artificial flowers and in
August Vanessa also began designing hats. She obviously enjoyed this kind
of work. About her flowers she wrote to Roger, 'It's rather amusing work
and they generally seem to me to be much more beautiful than God's
attempts! – I don't imitate Him of course but take hints sometimes.'[6] In
the autumn of 1916 there were further plans for amateur dressmaking,
mainly in order to provide work for Barbara Bagenal and Faith Henderson,
and the mistakes of the first attempt gave rise to a new idea, explained by
Vanessa, which, however, never materialized:

> Also I thought the reason it was a failure was really because Miss Joy didn't
> make well enough and that they must be properly trained as it's so compara-
> tively easy to make for oneself or a friend but without training I'm sure one
> can't make for someone like Lalla [Mme Vandervelde, the wife of a Belgian
> Socialist politician and a close friend of Roger's] . . . I also consulted Mary
> about it as I thought her help would be valuable – she was very strongly in
> favour of our inventing one kind of dress only, something very simple, not
> fashionable – which would have to be very well cut – which could be made in
> different stuffs and colours and have all kinds of different borders and edges
> and embroideries so as to get variety but make it always one dress which would
> get known as the Omega dress. She thought also we could have knitted caps
> and woolwork hats such as I made once. She thought the mistake we made
> before was in trying to be ordinary dressmakers as well as having one's own
> stuffs etc. as she said any good dressmaker could beat us at that, but that we
> ought to get this one kind of dress, with our own choice of colour and detail,
> known and sold for about £3 or £4. She thought that would be very successful.
> The difficulty would be to get the really good pattern to start with, but that
> Faith would have to do.[7]

'Study' by E. McKnight Kauffer, from 'Woodcuts by Various Artists', 1918.

At the same time as Vanessa's show of costumes in June 1915 the Omega held an exhibition of woodcuts by Roald Kristian, and in the same year it embarked on another new venture, book production. The first title was *Simpson's Choice*, by Arthur Clutton-Brock, the art critic of *The Times*, published with woodcuts by Roald Kristian. In February 1916 came *Men of Europe*, Roger Fry's translation of some poems from Pierre-Jean Jouve's *Vous êtes hommes*, followed by R. C. Trevelyan's translation of *Lucretius on Death* in 1917 and *Woodcuts by Various Artists* in 1918.

This last had originally been intended for publication by Leonard and Virginia Woolf's new Hogarth Press, but Vanessa disagreed with Leonard about who should retain artistic control and the production was taken over by the Omega. It included woodcuts by Roger, Duncan, Vanessa, Roald Kristian, Edward Wolfe, Simon Bussy and McKnight Kauffer.

In November 1915 Omega carpets, furniture and pottery, and also five works by Henri Gaudier-Brzeska, were included in an exhibition of Roger's paintings at the Alpine Club Gallery.

Vanessa's time at Eleanor in the spring had given her some new ideas about how to live, which were perhaps stimulated by her deeply felt antagonism to the war. She wrote to Clive from Sussex that it was 'very nice and peaceful with no front door bells and no telephones and no one unexpectedly to dinner'[8]; and, back in London, to Roger: 'I sometimes feel more than ever how nice it would be to live in the country, but I see

'Harlequinade' by Mark Gertler, cut by Roger Fry, from 'Woodcuts by Various Artists', 1918.

Three of the illustrations from 'Woodcuts by Various Artists': left, 'The Cup' and 'Still Life' by Roger Fry; above, 'Black Cat' by Simon Bussy.

that can't be done just yet, perhaps not till the end of the war. I think I shall really do it some day though.'⁹ In August she accompanied Duncan Grant and Maynard Keynes to Bosham in Sussex to stay in a house called The Grange, which she described as

> a genteel little house in which I don't feel very much at home yet. It's furnished in drab colours – none of those wonderful real lodging house arrangements of colour – and it's all very prim and clean and tidy. However it's beginning to look less so and I daresay we shall soon knock it about a bit with the children's help . . .¹⁰

'Knocking a house about a bit' soon came to include painting the walls with murals and designs. This was obviously an Omega habit, but also one which Duncan had practised for some time. In 1910 he had decorated Maynard's rooms at King's College, Cambridge, and in 1911, when working on the Borough Polytechnic murals, he and Frederick Etchells had decorated Maynard's room at Brunswick Square with a scene showing a street accident. In the first floor drawing room, helped by Adrian Stephen, he had done an abstract mural in reds and yellows of a game of tennis.

Vanessa's reaction to dingy houses was not one of offence at bad taste so much as a feeling of being stifled by all the connections with Victorian conventions. If a house could be made free, through decoration, for family life and for work, then so much the better, even if the final effect was somewhat improvised. This hatred of Victorian interiors, representing claustrophobic family life, was an important binding factor among Vanessa's friends. Roger's family had moved in 1887 from Highgate to a house near Kensington Gardens in Bayswater. Roger was then at Cambridge and disliked the rigid Quaker vigilance of his family home. Three years earlier the Strachey family had moved nearby to 69 Lancaster Gate, where until 1905 Duncan spent his school holidays. In 1922 Lytton Strachey read to the Memoir Club – the circle of friends which Clive Bell christened 'Bloomsbury' – an essay entitled 'Lancaster Gate' which encapsulates the kind of horror these young people came to associate with their parental homes, full of well-meaning relatives, maiden aunts and visiting friends of the family. Home, to Lytton Strachey,

> was size gone wrong, size pathological; it was a house afflicted with elephantiasis that one found one had entered, when, having passed through the front door and down the narrow dark passage with its ochre walls and its tessellated floor of magenta and indigo tiles, one looked upwards and saw the staircase

twisting steeply up its elongated well – spiralling away into a thin infinitude, until far above, one's surprised vision came upon a dome of pink and white glass, which yet one judged, with an unerring instinct, was not the top – no, not nearly, nearly the top.[11]

His later home, Ham Spray House, was decorated with murals by Dora Carrington; Vanessa and Duncan were to be responsible for transforming the rooms of many of their friends. It is perhaps not surprising that Roger rejected the grand interiors and lavish upholstery which were *de rigueur* among collectors of Old Master paintings, for he disliked the power of wealth he had seen in America. He was little concerned with the connection between art and money and this must have endeared him all the more to his friends.

In 1915 the first anxieties about conscription had arisen; Vanessa and Duncan received inside information on this subject from Maynard, who had joined the Treasury earlier that year. It was also from him that they heard, in October, of the true conditions at the Front. Keynes had been talking to soldiers convalescing in Cambridge who gave him the first evidence of shell-shock and trauma following bayonet charges; none of them wanted to return to the Front. Duncan, Clive, Lytton Strachey and David Garnett were pacifists, as were many of their circle of friends. Roger, as a Quaker, was exempt from conscription. Duncan, Lytton and David Garnett had agreed that they would sooner go to prison than be forced to fight; meanwhile, they were pinning their hopes on the introduction of a conscience clause. Vanessa herself became involved with the work of the No Conscription Fellowship, of which her brother Adrian was secretary, and with the National Council for Civil Liberties. They all believed that conscription was a gross infringement of individual liberty and Vanessa even had vague hopes that the threatened legislation would force trade union leaders to call for action to put a stop to conscription and to the war itself. She felt that the social world they had known was disappearing and wondered whether she could bear to stay in England once the war came to an end.

The Military Service Act was introduced on 5 January 1916 and came into direct effect two months later. Pacifists and those opposed to the war now had to account for themselves. On Maynard's advice, in order to help his case against conscription Duncan moved from London to take up work as an agricultural labourer, renting Wissett Lodge, near Halesworth in Suffolk, which was at the disposal of his father following the death of an elderly relative. The year 1916 was a disastrous one for the Allies in the management of the war: every day British families of all classes received telegrams reporting the death of a father, son, brother or lover, and there was a great deal of bad feeling against conscientious objectors and those who did not support the war. Those actively against it could do little to state their case, and were often made to look as though they were culpably indifferent to the carnage and suffering. In May Duncan applied to a tribunal for exemption as a conscientious objector, but was refused and had to appeal. His application to become a War Artist was also refused. Of his attitude at the time David Garnett wrote:

> Duncan took the line that he belonged to a tiny minority and that his views differed *in toto* from the majority on almost every subject. His opinions would never be attended to, and he would never fight for those of the majority, particularly as he believed it was always morally wrong to employ violence.[12]

(Much later, in 1950, it was the majority position that he was rejecting when he declined a C.B.E.)

At Wissett Duncan had the company of Vanessa and her children – she had gone down with him to keep house – and soon that of David Garnett, who came to work with him on the farm. Vanessa settled quickly and appeared to be more content than she had been for some time. Pre-occupations with art came again to the fore in her frequent letters to Roger:

> I do no painting and curiously enough so far have not wished to though I think a good deal about it while I dig and do things. I daresay its [*sic*] the best thing in the world for one's work to have to put it entirely out of the question for a few months. After all one never has a holiday unless one does some other work to make painting impossible.
>
> I have beginnings of wanting to paint again though but I think I shall paint less and less from life and more and more from drawings. I want more and more to make pictures like objects in some way and yet believe it is useless to invent. I want to paint unrealistic realistic works. I daresay there is a word in German for it . . . You will think I've gone to seed . . . Anyhow I'm never going to live in the town again. I can't think why anyone does. Life is a round of pleasures in the country – on a fine day and today has been gloriously hot.[13]

In June, when Lytton Strachey came to stay, she wrote: 'we have had the usual discussions on all subjects but I think they find us all rather stupid from being in the country'.[14] Vanessa was still thinking hard about painting and obviously tried to explain herself to Lytton:

But Lytton admitted in the end that he had very little sense of anything but the human interest in painting. He is very suspicious of our attitude about art and thinks we don't understand our own feelings and are trying to prove a theory. I, on the other hand, think him almost entirely dramatic in his appreciations. I mean I believe he only feels character and relationships of character and has no conception of the form it's all being made into.[15]

Vanessa and Duncan's removal from London obviously meant that they could take little part in the affairs of the Omega, which was not doing well. In February, Roger wrote to his friend Charles Vildrac, 'I go on painting and working at the Omega, which threatens to die but does not die, but I feel this terrible lack of confidence in whatever I do. There is no more future.'[16] Roger's antidote to depression had always been hard work and in the spring he threw himself into a commission that the Omega received to decorate Arthur Ruck's house at No. 4 Berkeley Street in London. He was helped on this by Nina Hamnett, Roald Kristian and Moucha Courtney, a half-Russian, half-Spanish painter who worked at the Omega. The mural decorations were based on the theme of the London Underground, and Fry also designed a large circular rug and some inlaid tables. The house was the subject of an article in *Colour* magazine in June 1916. The 'Scenes from Contemporary London Life' depicted on the walls of the landing showed a lady ascending the steps from the Underground, with a newspaper stall in the background, rendered with no attempt at perspective, in tones of crimson, orange, yellow, purple, pink, brown and a dull green. Compared to the other illustrations in *Colour* of work by Augustus John, Paul Nash, McKnight Kauffer and C. W. R. Nevinson, the colours stand out somewhat garishly and the large, plainly delineated figures seem a little imposing for a domestic interior. Louise Gordon-Stables, the author of the article, concluded, however, that the scheme was a beneficial shock to the artistic perceptions.

In February 1916 the Omega had held an exhibition of paintings and in August it showed the work of Alvaro Guevara, a young Chilean painter who was studying at the Slade. But there were pressing financial worries. Roger wrote to Vanessa at the beginning of August:

At the meeting of the Omega the accountant took a gloomy view of things. It appears that our expenses are about £360 a year on the lowest possible basis and this would require sales of £90 a month to cover. I doubt if we average £40. So the thing does seem rather hopeless as I don't think there can be any great revival after the war.[17]

Vanessa, who now took little part in the affairs of the Omega, replied to this letter:

> I think in that case – and as you don't want to continue it in London – it ought to stop, oughtn't it? I don't see why you should put more of your money in. I should have thought it would be better to return Bernard Shaw his share of the remains and keep your own and perhaps do pottery with it which you could certainly sell privately as you do pictures or at some shop couldn't you. However I daresay I shall see you before this need be decided.[18]

The Omega did rally slightly and at the end of the year Roger's friend Lalla Vandervelde commissioned the Workshops to decorate her flat in Rossetti Garden Mansions, Chelsea. To some extent her friendship compensated Roger for the loss of Vanessa. She admired the Omega and had promised to try and find commissions among her Belgian friends.

Roger was still not reconciled to Vanessa's new way of life. In June he had written to her:

> You are the only one I really want to talk to intimately, so I'm developing bit by bit a habit of solitude. I go to the Omega in the morning, see to business with Winnie and then come back and paint all day till evening, and now most often spend that alone. It's better than making believe with people, and in a few years I'll have got such a crust that no one will break through. It may break down, but it's my plan of life just now . . . I am myself again now you know after all those years of not being. All sorts of things I'd suppressed because they didn't meet with anything in you are coming back. It's a very queer state. I don't like myself any better but I'm no longer disgusted with it for not being exactly like you or what you like or admire.[19]

The following week Virginia and Leonard went to stay with Roger and reported to a friend:

> Roger, I thought rather melancholy. He talked a lot about old age, and the horrors of loneliness; the poor man can't make up his mind to have done with youth, and his attempts to keep with the young are rather pathetic.[20]

He was then fifty.

Vanessa was preoccupied with other matters. Duncan and David had appealed to the tribunal dealing with the claims of conscientious objectors; after a long wait a decision came in their favour, but with the reservation that Duncan could not work what was essentially his own land. Vanessa went looking for a house near Firle, in Sussex, where they had heard of a farmer who would employ the two friends. Firle was near Asheham and

Virginia remembered a house she had noticed there during a walk. Vanessa went to see it and soon made arrangements to rent Charleston, an old farmhouse that had been a guesthouse, with a pond in front of it and a walled garden to the side, close under the Downs. In October 1916, after a stay at Eleanor, Duncan, David, Vanessa, Julian and Quentin removed to Charleston, where Duncan and Vanessa were to stay for the rest of their lives.

'Dahlias' by Vanessa Bell, from 'Woodcuts by Various Artists', 1918.

4

The ending of the Omega

THE commission to decorate Lalla Vandervelde's flat gave Roger a chance to experiment with new techniques. He undertook most of the work himself and used the results as the basis for an article in *Colour* in April 1917, entitled 'The Artist as Decorator'. In it he applied the same reasoning to the decoration of walls that he had expressed in relation to objects in the preface to the Omega catalogue, and found a place for the artist in the humble occupation of house-painting.

> I am assuming that we call in the artist, not in order to paint pictures on the walls after the fashion of the fresco painters of the Renaissance, but merely to paint the walls in some purely abstract and formal way. Now our artist may be able, merely out of the contrast of two or three pure colours applied in simple rectangular shapes, to transform a room completely, giving it a new feeling of space or dignity or richness. In fact, he can underline as it were the actual proportional beauty of the architecture or counteract its architectural defectiveness.

He went on to describe Lalla Vandervelde's flat:

> The walls were spaced out with pilasters of a pale petunia colour, made with aniline dye, put on with a smallish brush – as the dye dries in instantly and the brush strokes overlapped, the result was a peculiar moiré effect, which relieved the pilasters against the flatter colour of the rest of the wall. This was done in pure raw sienna, also applied with separate brush strokes, which gave the whole surface an agreeable vivacity.

He also described effects of marbling and of panelling, using rectangles of hand-painted paper:

> Each panel . . . differs very slightly, but still distinctly in quality from the next, and the whole surface has a play and vivacity which are essential to the effect of richness and solidity.[1]

The success of the room as a whole relied upon the artist's confidence in applying individual brush strokes, creating an environment sensitive to the painter's technique. Roger was also to use this technique when he came to decorate his new house in Dalmeny Avenue in 1919. He may well have been inspired by Duncan and Vanessa's experiments with abstract and collage paintings during 1915. These relied as much upon the dynamism of the brush strokes as upon the juxtaposition of harmonizing and opposing colours. Vanessa and Duncan, too, were later to use Roger's method of covering large wall spaces in this simple and effective manner. Roger was after the same kind of almost improvised finish that he had sought in his pottery; and, indeed, he often took time off from Lalla Vandervelde's commission to go down to Poole where he was working on plates, soup tureens, vegetable dishes and dinner sets in black, dull yellow, green or purple glazes.

Another event at the end of 1916 helped to revitalize Roger's flagging spirits, when he organized an Omega stand for the Arts and Crafts Exhibition Society show at the Royal Academy. The Society, which had held triannual exhibitions since 1890, was founded in 1888 by a splinter group of the Art Workers' Guild, including such central Arts and Crafts designers as Walter Crane, Lewis F. Day, W. R. Lethaby, W. A. S. Benson and William de Morgan. In 1916 William Morris's daughter, May, was on the committee. The Omega exhibited in the company of such artists as Charles Rennie Mackintosh and his wife Margaret, W. A. S. Benson, and the jewellers and silversmiths J. Paul Cooper, Arthur Gaskin, Edward Spencer and Phoebe and Harold Stabler. Their fine craftsmanship obviously showed up the poor workmanship of the Omega products and it was small wonder that the organizers were loath to include the Omega. Their reluctance to accept design as an end in itself raised Roger's hackles, and he derived great enjoyment from forcing himself upon them. In September he wrote to Vanessa:

> I had a deputation of the Arts and Crafts yesterday at the Omega. Three sour and melancholy elderly hypocrites, full of sham modesty and noble sentiments. I was very firm with them and they've decided to offer me a corner of one of their galleries. I said I would only exhibit if I considered the space adequate. Of course poor men they couldn't help admitting how good most of the things were – while inwardly hating them and me all the time. They represent to perfection the hideous muddleheaded sentimentality of the English – wanting to mix in elevated moral feeling with everything. I wish I could tell you in writing the preposterous phrases they used.[2]

Two days later he wrote to his mother:

I've really been quite hard worked with the Omega of late. I'm to have an exhibit of our things in the great arts and crafts exhibition at the R.A. Isn't that amusing? But what was most amusing was the way in which the good people tried to leave me out and failed. I told them that it was a matter of complete indifference to me whether we showed or not, but that if we didn't show I would publicly contest any claim that their exhibition was representative of British applied art – whereupon they thought that the lesser evil was to give me a section to show in. I am now arranging it and hope to make some effect mainly by being so much soberer and more austere than my neighbours.[3]

So Roger had his way, but his offensive tactics can hardly have endeared him to the members of the committee who were still a powerful and popular force in contemporary design, through their official links in the Design and Industries Association and through their art-school connections.

When he got to the Royal Academy in October, he found, however, that he was not entirely alone in his taste:

Just thro' the doorway from where I was I saw some quite jolly textiles and asked the girls who were putting them up what they were – they said oh this is only a commercial exhibit of things made for the negroes. I said they seemed very nice – whereupon they burst out in horror at the general exhibition and said how pleased they were to see the Omega things which looked like something at last. So we're in good company. The rest is such incredible lunatic humbug and genteel nonsense as you could hardly believe possible.[4]

To give the Arts and Crafts designers their due, they did not just forget him with a sigh of relief once the exhibition closed. In March 1917 they asked him to speak at a meeting of the Art Workers' Guild. Roger was unabashed:

I gave them a terrific sermon about their attitude to art and their want of any clear thought about it and their desire to make everything moral and what not. They were as meek as a lamb and I found I could say just what I wanted. It ended in them asking me to explain what I meant by form and their asking questions. Altogether it was rather a triumph considering their attitude in the past. But of course they are so fundamentally stupid that I don't suppose its much good. I denounced futurism among other things and Nevinson was much shocked. He thought we agreed about art and he saw we differed entirely. However he was quite nice about it . . .[5]

While he rejected the established design world, Roger welcomed the unusual, and in the spring he championed a young teacher who had come to London with a portfolio of the work she had been doing with her pupils to try and find a job. Marion Richardson was a friend of his sister Margery, who was principal of a women's university hostel in Birmingham, and herself a remarkable woman. When Miss Richardson found herself unable to get a job, she called at the Omega to see if Roger could help her. She was already aware of the Omega's style, for Margery had many furnishings from the Workshops. It is indicative of Roger's true values that he was prepared to put all his energy into helping an insignificant art teacher who he felt was on the right track. He described Miss Richardson's method to Vanessa:

> When she came to teach she invented methods of making the children put down their own visualizations – 'drawing' with eyes shut etc – I assure you they're simply marvellous. Many of them are a kind of cross between early miniatures and Seurat but all are absolutely individual and original. Everyone who's seen them is amazed. [Augustus] John was in and said quite truly it makes one feel horribly jealous. I long to see what you'll say. Anyway here's an inexhaustible supply of real primitive art and real vision which the government suppresses at a cost of hundreds of thousands of pounds. If the world weren't the most crazily topsy turvey place one would never believe it possible.[6]

In many ways this was the idea at the heart of the Atelier Martine, where Poiret wanted above all for his schoolgirls to avoid any formal art training and just to transcribe their impressions directly in terms of design. The idea was not new to Roger; in 'An Essay in Aesthetics', first published in 1909 and reprinted in *Vision and Design* in 1920, he had written:

> That the graphic arts are the expression of the imaginative life rather than a copy of actual life might be guessed from observing children. Children, if left to themselves, never, I believe, copy what they see, never, as we say, 'draw from nature', but express, with a delightful freedom and sincerity, the mental images which make up their own imaginative lives.[7]

Roger also wrote of Marion Richardson to his daughter Pamela, whose own childhood drawings may well have been the inspiration for the foregoing observations:

> I think all she does is to make them put down the composition with their eyes shut and then work from that. The things are simply too lovely for anything. They illustrate homes and scenes of their lives and all sorts of things . . . They're quite different to the things artist's children like you and the little Johns and Gills do, and I daresay they'd never come to be artists, but the imagination is astonishing.[8]

Roger exhibited the drawings at the Omega and showed them to the Minister of Education in an effort to change the official attitude towards art teaching. He also wrote an article for *The Burlington Magazine*. A second, retrospective, exhibition was held at the Omega in February 1919, and by 1922 a place had been found for Miss Richardson's talents after Margery Fry sent her to see Dr Hamblin Smith in Birmingham, who was an originator of educational work in prisons – a subject to which Margery devoted much of her life. Marion Richardson was employed to teach painting to young boy prisoners at Winson Green.

In February or March 1917 the Omega Club was founded. The subscription was 5s. and the club met weekly on Thursday evenings in Fitzroy Square. Luminaries such as Clive Bell, Lytton Strachey, Shaw, Yeats and Arnold Bennett attended these meetings. One of the early entertainments was 'War and Peace: A Dramatic Fantasia' by G. L. Dickinson, performed with marionettes made by Winifred Gill. The proceeds went to aid the many Belgian refugees who had settled near Fitzroy Square.

While Roger was writing to Vanessa with news of the Omega, her letters to him were full of her life at Charleston. Soon after moving in she write enthusiastically: 'It really is so lovely that I must show it to you soon. It's absolutely perfect I think . . . The Omega dinner service looks most lovely on the dresser.'⁹ The countryside around the farm was familiar to her, for Asheham was nearby, and, for the duration of the war at least, her future was settled. Despite their isolation and the hard work that Duncan and David had to put in for Mr Hecks, their new employer, Charleston was a haven after the anxieties of waiting for the tribunal to hand down its decision.

Vanessa's first priority was the house itself. She had had an inkling of her powers at Eleanor and Wissett Lodge, and now the precepts of the Omega could be followed to full advantage. In his autobiography, David Garnett looked back on this time with fondness:

> Then some furniture was brought down from 46 Gordon Square, other pieces were bought in Lewes and these with rare exceptions were astounding objects, bargains which attracted Duncan or Vanessa because of their strange shapes and low prices . . . Both . . . appeared to believe that the inherent horror of any badly designed and constructed piece of furniture could be banished forever by decoration.¹⁰

This was the beginning of a lifetime's hard work. In the winter of 1916 she wrote to Roger, 'I hope to carry out the idea I have always had of bedrooms with the minimum of furniture – but it's odd how it creeps on one – even here one finds chests of drawers unexpectedly.'[11]

During the following spring she was busy on a project of her own:

> I have started a large picture meant as a decoration for one of the walls in the garden sitting room. There's very little in the picture and it's mostly one colour – or two – Yellow ochre and a greenish grey. The subject is principally floor with a bath and a semi-nude female . . . and the pond seen through the window. As it's 6 ft by 5 ft 6 it will I'm afraid tend to be monotonous.[12]

> I've been working at my big bath picture and am rather excited about that. I've taken out the woman's chemise and in consequence she is quite nude and much more decent.[13]

While Duncan and David worked on the farm Vanessa had many varied occupations. There were frequent visits to Leonard and Virginia over the Downs, although Leonard felt that Julian and Quentin were too noisy for Virginia's nerves. Virginia certainly didn't appear to share his view and exulted in her descriptions of Vanessa's new life, feeling it to be all of a part with her view of her sister's character. In April Virginia wrote separately to two friends about the Charleston household:

> Nessa and Duncan came over yesterday, having previously washed themselves; and then went back in a storm late at night to help ducklings out of their eggs, for they were heard quacking inside, and couldn't break through. Nessa seems to have slipped civilization off her back, and splashes about entirely nude, without shame, and enormous spirit. Indeed, Clive now takes up the line that she has ceased to be a presentable lady – I think it all works admirably.[14]

> Nessa is 4 miles on the other side of the down, living like an old hen wife among ducks, chickens and children. She never wants to put on proper clothes again – even a bath seems to distress her. Her children are for ever asking her questions and she invents all sorts of answers, never having known very accurately about facts.[15]

In May the Omega held an exhibition which was largely the result of Duncan and Vanessa's activities at Wissett Lodge the previous spring. It was called 'Copies and Translations' and included copies mainly of early Florentine paintings, although Mark Gertler contributed a copy of a Cézanne and Moucha Courtney sent one of a Derain painting. Duncan had already copied the work of both Masaccio and Piero della Francesca when in Florence with his mother in the winter of 1904, but it was Roger

who had led Vanessa to a new appreciation of the inherent qualities of
early Italian painting. Vanessa contributed a Giotto and a Bronzino,
Duncan an Antonio Pollaiuolo and a detail of a Piero della Francesca,
Roger a Cimabue and also an early copy of a Piero di Cosimo by his wife,
Helen.

Vanessa had begun copying Italian paintings while at Wissett Lodge
and Roger had obviously been delighted that she was at last showing more
than a cursory interest in the art that had been his first love. He encouraged
her by sending reproductions from the large collection of photographs he
kept for reference for his writings and lectures, the invaluable tool of the
art expert. In May 1916 she wrote to him:

> Duncan and I have both begun what seems too hopeless an undertaking copy-
> ing minute reproductions of Fra Angelico about 10 times as big on the walls
> of my bedroom in watercolours. I think it *is* rather hopeless. Duncan hasn't
> been able to do much to his but it is very lovely, while mine which is further
> advanced is neither myself nor Fra Angelico and I'm rather desperate about it.
> The original is a most lovely design. It's the Visitation – with the two figures
> meeting by a doorway and a girl looking on and a man waiting nearby. It's an
> extraordinary design but I'm very bad at copying though I rather enjoy doing
> it. I think one gets to understand pictures in a way one can't otherwise.[16]

And again in the summer:

> I have been working hard at the copy of the Giotto. Duncan thinks it's going
> to be better than the other as it's on a larger scale in which I'm more at home.
> I am rather excited about it as I enjoy doing it so much. For some reason I feel
> nearly as free as if I were painting on my own account. I have quite changed
> the colour scheme which you mayn't approve of as I suspect it's not so like the
> original, but when I looked at it again it all seemed to suggest something much
> paler than it had at first. I have made the sky a pale, yellowish green and behind
> the figures a sort of raw sienna and they are in dark blacks and pale greys and
> pinks and reds and the building is pink. There's no blue in it.[17]

Years later Duncan explained to John Rothenstein the value he found in
copying paintings which he admired:

> When I first came to know him at the Stracheys Simon Bussy urgently impressed
> upon me the value of making copies and I've always followed his advice. I
> don't try to make exact copies but interpretations. I agree with Bussy that there
> is a great deal to be learnt from this practice. It isn't the painting that one does
> before another painting that teaches one. The real idea behind copying is to
> induce one to look at a picture for a long time. Even if you're a painter and

deeply interested, it is difficult to look for very long and it is much easier if one is doing something.[18]

Roger himself experienced the same learning process as Duncan and Vanessa. He wrote to Vanessa in April 1917 that he had been copying the figure of St Francis from a fresco by Cimabue in Assisi and that he found

> Cimabue more wonderful than ever . . . I had never really studied that before at least not with enlightened eyes and find that what I thought before were the weaknesses of early incapacity are really the results of a sensibility one had never understood . . . what's so wonderful – when one begins to study the forms in detail one finds just the kind of purposeful distortion and pulling of planes that you get in Greco and Cézanne and the same kind of sequence in the contours.[19]

His 'enlightened eyes' were the result of his appreciation of Post-Impressionism. Despite his disappointment in his own painting, the true source of his criticism was his ardent involvement with the painterly activity, the practical concern with the design of a canvas which he felt released the true vision of the artist. And of course nothing could be better than to find that his friends were also discovering links between the early Italians and the Post-Impressionists.

The Copies and Translations exhibition was a good example of the internal loyalty of the Omega. The artists stood to earn money from work which they had undertaken solely for their own interests, and at the same time the public was made aware of what the true concerns of a working artist might include. Roger was unwilling to use the Omega to cater for public taste, preferring to try and educate an audience which was ignorant of what artists actually did with their time. The show was not a success, although Maynard loyally bought one of Duncan's paintings. The exhibition also brought other problems to light. Both Walter Sickert and Nina Hamnett had promised to contribute, but eventually did not; Mark Gertler delivered his canvas after the show had opened. This was the first Omega exhibition to suffer a complete boycott by the critics, which meant that it received no publicity. In the first week after it opened on 11 May, only ten people visited the show. Sickert thought there was a 'political' motivation – the unpopularity of the Omega made evident. Roger was as much angry as disillusioned.

There were further frictions in the following month when Duncan and Vanessa took on a private commission to decorate Mary Hutchinson's house without going through the Omega, which needed the publicity as much as the money. As directors, Roger felt, Duncan and Vanessa should at least have considered how the Omega would suffer from such an act. Vanessa argued that Duncan had not in fact worked on any Omega commission for about two years and that he had not earned enough money from the Workshops to make it worth his while to pass other commissions through the firm. Roger was understandably upset at the public acknowledgment of the Workshops' decline and privately distressed by this final evidence that his original plans were ebbing away.

Vanessa had her own problems. During the summer Charleston received a stream of visitors and she had constant difficulties finding adequate help to cope with them. She couldn't get up to London to talk to Roger about the Hutchinson commission because she had no one to look after the children, especially Julian who was old enough to need an intelligent companion to keep him safely occupied. By the time the fracas with Roger had been smoothed over, Vanessa was in trouble with Mary Hutchinson because of a letter in which Vanessa had slightly disparaged her. As Clive's mistress, Mary was extremely sensitive to Vanessa's opinion. Vanessa pleaded that her comments had been caused by the pressures of being overrun with visitors, and Mary was mollified.

By August, when life was running a little more smoothly, other preoccupations came to the fore. Vanessa wrote to Roger asking for any mosaic left over from the one he and Duncan had done at Durbins in 1911, explaining that

> We are busy, when it's not pouring too hard, making a small cemented place to sit out on and we're going to make a small inlaid piece of mosaic of odd bits of china, glass, etc. in the centre and also a narrow border round the edge . . . The border will be only about 3 or 4 inches wide and 5 ft square so not much would be wanted only I think one ought to have some one or two colours running through the medley of bits of china, etc.[20]

Roger was continually involved in the Charleston establishment, helping Vanessa to find servants, a governess, a tutor when she had the idea of starting a small school there, and sending books on science for Julian. He took a great interest in the planting out of the garden, as did Maynard, who helped enthusiastically with the weeding when he came to stay. In September, Vanessa and Barbara Bagenal were helping Duncan to complete his costumes for Jacques Copeau's New York production of Maeterlinck's *Pelléas et Mélisande.*

1 'Couple Dancing', a design by Vanessa Bell for a panel which hung at first floor level outside the Omega Workshops from 1913.

2 Reverse side of the Omega signboard, painted by Duncan Grant in 1915 (see the Frontispiece).

3 'Bathers in a Landscape',
painted screen by Vanessa Bell,
1913.

4 Design for a screen by
Wyndham Lewis, 1913.

Two marquetry trays made by Kallenborn & Sons: on the left, 'The Wrestlers' by Henri Gaudier-Brzeska; on the right, 'Elephant' by Duncan Grant.

Painted lampstands with silk shades.

OMEGA WORKSHOPS

Left (top to bottom) and above:

7   'White', printed linen designed by Vanessa Bell in 1913.

8   'Cracow', jacquard woven fabric designed by Vanessa Bell and produced by A. H. Lee in 1913.

9   'Margery', printed linen possibly designed by Roger Fry, 1913.

10   'Mechtilde', printed linen designed by Frederick Etchells in 1913.

11   'Pamela', printed linen designed by Vanessa Bell in 1913.

2 *Winifred Gill (right) and Nina Hamnett modelling dresses at the Omega.*

13   One of three rugs designed for General Sir Ian and Lady Hamilton in 1914.

14   Design for a rug
by Roald Kristian.

15 *Bed painted by Roger Fry for Lalla Vandervelde, 1916–17.*

16 *Painted corner washstand.*

17, 18 *Design for a marquetry cupboard, and the cupboard itself. (The top is not original.)*

19 *Marquetry dressing table made by J. Kallenborn & Sons in 1919.*

20 Painted table and
embroidered firescreen; and a
caned chair painted red in
imitation of lacquer, designed by
Roger Fry for the Omega and
made by Dryad Ltd (compare the
chairs in pl. XV) The screen,
formerly attributed to the
Omega, was not made in the
Workshops.

21 Chair with needlepoint back
designed by Roger Fry.

22, 23 *Two vases with painted overglaze decoration.*

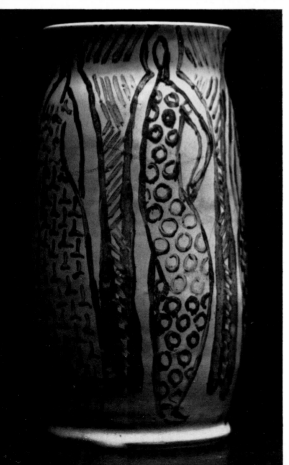

24 *Dinner plate, bowl and jug in white tin-glazed earthenware by Roger Fry, c.1915, produced at the Poole Pottery.*

25 Two plates with painted overglaze decoration, 1913. The one
on the left is by Wyndham Lewis, that on the right by Duncan Grant.

26 Two plates with painted overglaze decoration by Duncan Grant, 1913.

27 *The dining room in Charles Rennie Mackintosh's Willow Tearooms, Glasgow, 1904.*

28 *Drawing for a dining room by Paul Poiret's Atelier Martine, 1924.*

29 *The Cadena Café at 59 Westbourne Grove, London, decorated* ▷ *by the Omega in 1914.*

30 *Design by the Wiener Werkstätte for the 'Cabarett Fledermaus', Vienna, 1907.*

31 *Mural of a game of tennis by Duncan Grant in Adrian Stephen's room at 38 Brunswick Square, London, 1912.*

32 *Mural decorations by the Omega, c. 1913–14.*

33 *Shutters painted by Vanessa Bell for Barbara Bagenal.*

34 *Bookcase painted by Duncan Grant, part of Duncan and Vanessa's decorations for Clive Bell at 50 Gordon Square, London, in 1927.*

35 *Large embroidered music stool designed by Duncan Grant and worked by his mother, Mrs Ethel Grant, in 1925. It was included in the Independent Gallery exhibition 'Modern Needlework' in 1925 and is now at Charleston (see pl. XIV).*

The many letters written at this time show the endless chatter that went on over the business of arranging Charleston satisfactorily. Vanessa made a variety of demands on Roger:

> If it's easy it would be very nice if you could bring the Italian pot . . . Could you also bring the Cézanne? As for flowers any are very welcome. I want to make the new paths and beds you suggested so there will be lots of room for all kinds of things. Pinks, irises and anything you have to spare. Also if you can we should be very glad of thyme and sage – but I daresay you haven't got those to spare.[21]

Virginia, too, observed the endless activities of the household with some amusement and wrote to Lady Ottoline Morrell, who had her own rival establishment of conscientious objectors at Garsington in Oxfordshire, where Clive was supposedly working on the Morrells' farm, 'It is very lovely here, and we meet Nessa and Duncan and have picnics on the downs; they seem perfectly happy, painting, making jam, getting all their own vegetables, and yesterday Nessa went to Brighton and bought a donkey.'[22]

The hectic summer had, however, slightly shaken Vanessa's confidence, and in a warm letter she turned again for reassurance to Roger. The problems that had arisen between them since their break-up could be easily forgotten and the underlying devotion they had for one another was still readily accessible. As Roger had once remarked, he always knew there would come a time when Vanessa would need his special understanding of her again. In return he fervently reiterated the advice he had always given her, showing no resentment of the fact that he had suffered from her success in following it.

> Oh, why do I admire you? My dear, it would take ages to tell you all I do admire you for; but you see, I think you go straight for the things that are worthwhile – you have done such an extraordinarily difficult thing without any fuss; cut thro' all the conventions, kept friends with a pernickety creature like Clive, got quit of me and yet kept me your devoted friend, got all the things you need for your own development and yet managed to be a splendid mother – no, you really can't wonder. You give one a sense of security, of something solid and real in a shifting world . . . Then to your marvellous practical power, which has, of course, really a quality of great imagination in it, because your efficiency comes without effort or worry or fuss. No, I don't think you need ever doubt yourself. You have a genius in your life as well as in your art and both are rare things, so you can feel pretty well pleased with yourself. I, who have no trace of genius anyhow, can't help a deep envy of your gifts. But I do

admit that it's really the nicest thing to feel that you care to tell me your worries and difficulties again.[23]

Roger sometimes tended to dramatize to Vanessa the loneliness and isolation he experienced both privately and at the Omega: his feelings of worthlessness were hardly shared by those who knew him. Despite Vanessa's private struggles to free herself from their relationship, her friends and family continued to show a strong affection and admiration for him. Earlier in the year Clive had observed to Vanessa, 'Roger is full of pictures and theories and more charming than ever. If I can be like that at the age of 50 what 2? 3? 4? I shall be content.'[24] (Roger was in fact fifty-one.) After the war, Virginia praised him equally: 'Roger is a miracle. And I need not expatiate upon his powers, though on a hot afternoon, after talking to Derain and seeing pictures all the morning, his incessant activities surprised me.'[25]

The winter of 1917 was difficult. The Germans were attempting to starve Britain by means of a submarine blockade, and food and fuel were in short supply. Vanessa had to postpone her idea of a school until rations would be available to feed her pupils, although she did invest in Belgian hares, a pig and some rabbits. Christmas was spent at Charleston, which Vanessa found a welcome relief from the rigours of being with her parents-in-law at Seend, but in January she had influenza. As a result of hard conditions on the farm Duncan lost weight and was extremely unwell, but had to wait for a letter from his London doctor before Mr Hecks could reduce his working day. Vanessa's studio was too cold to work in:

> This household is absolutely frozen . . . the cold is simply appalling. The only consolation is that it's so light. I sat and shivered, painting, as long as I could stand it all last week, then had a warm at the fire, and then another shiver. The only thing to do is paint the mantel pieces, so I have done the one in the studio.[26]

It was in this spirit that her decorations gradually came to cover the entire house. In February she painted the two doors flanking the mantelpiece in Duncan's bedroom with a vivacity of colour and line that belies her freezing surroundings. As she wrote to Virginia, 'It's awful being cut off from one's principal occupation isn't it? I'm thankful to be able to paint again. One gets that tetchy without it and is off one's balance.'[27]

In November 1917 the Omega had held its regular exhibition of paintings and works and in January 1918 Roger was commissioned to design the furniture and scenery for 'Mrs Bradley's drawing room' in Act 1 of

Israel Zangwill's play *Too Much Money*. After a tryout at the Royal
Theatre in Glasgow the play opened in London on 9 April at the Am-
bassadors Theatre and ran for sixty-two performances.

There were new frictions during 1918, this time within the Omega Club,
as Clive Bell wrote in a typically nonchalant letter to Vanessa:

> Duncan will possibly have told you that I raised some little objection to the
> predominance of the Stracheys and their creatures in the Omega Club; the
> Bloomsbury Basement. I hear the little people – Carrington, Faith, Barbara,
> Alix etc. – take great offence at what I said. Well let them. It's quite clear that
> under the existing rules we shall never get any new blood since the Strachey
> notion of an amusing club is one at which you meet in the evening all the same
> people that you spent the afternoon with. However, it doesn't matter a straw.[28]

(The 'little people' were Dora Carrington, Faith Henderson, Barbara
Bagenal and Alix Strachey.)

In the spring Vanessa found that she was pregnant. Only those closest
to her knew that the father was Duncan, and others were left to deduce
that the baby must be Clive's, who was quite happy about the deception.
When the baby was due, he suggested that he be there to make everything
appear respectable and to write the necessary letters. For many years most
people, including Angelica herself, assumed that Clive was her father.

Vanessa's pregnancy, however, greatly upset Roger. More than ever she
wanted to make Charleston her home and she became increasingly committed to her life there. In July Roger went to stay nearby at Bo-Peep
Farm. He preferred to see Vanessa by herself and still felt a certain resentment of Duncan's company, although the two men got along together
perfectly well when she was not present. But she saw no reason to have a
special time apart together. Tensions grew and relations between them
deteriorated. Roger felt that she was purposely dismissing him from her
life and that he was no longer special to her:

> I feel horribly lonely and at sea with the prospect of re-making my life. You
> see, my real life is with you and always has been since I got to know you. In
> comparison nothing else has counted – and tho' it's been a very poor little
> trickle of life that I've had since you left me, it still seems almost impossibly
> hard to cut that off. But even that little depends not on me, but on your caring
> to keep it going, and it looks to me as tho' you no longer had enough interest
> in me to do so.[29]

Vanessa was plainly confused by this attack and distressed by the strain
of his demands and his unwillingness to accept her new way of life now

that there was to be a further bond between Duncan and herself. She could not see the need for a friendship on his terms. However, she persevered, and in November wrote to him at length explaining that perhaps he expected something of her that had simply never been there – not something that she was coldly refusing him – and that having been in love with him she would always feel a special bond between them. This appears to have been the final phase of recrimination and explanation between Roger and Vanessa. Her pregnancy brought out all his worst fears of exclusion, but her reassurances, readily given only a month before Angelica's birth, did calm him in preparation for a new phase in both their lives. Roger became devoted to Duncan's child, who was born on Christmas Day 1918, and began to take full advantage of the pleasures Charleston offered.

An Omega exhibition of paintings was held in November 1918 and dresses were shown made of Omega fabrics by Gabrielle Soene, who was a friend of Modigliani in Paris. In December the work of McKnight Kauffer was on sale. Then in January 1919 Lalla Vandervelde returned to Belgium, and Roger missed both her company and her moral support for the Omega. It was mooted that he would design a stage set for a melodrama starring Lillah McCarthy (he spoke of decorations of 'phallic Gauguinesque flowers'), but nothing came of it. The previous autumn Roger had met Diaghilev at one of the many parties given for the Ballets Russes and it had been rumoured that Diaghilev might ask the Omega to design sets, with Duncan doing the costumes. This would not have been unlikely, for since the Ballets Russes had settled in Monte Carlo Diaghilev increasingly commissioned artists such as Picasso, Braque, Rouault and Derain to design sets, and Duncan was highly regarded in Paris as a result of his work for Jacques Copeau. But that idea, too, came to nothing.

On Boxing Day Roger went to see the ballet *Contes de Fées* and thought Michel Larionov's sets were 'marvellous'. Larionov was a Russian painter who worked with Diaghilev in Paris. Roger published an article on him in *The Burlington Magazine* and in February 1919 exhibited a selection of his designs, along with a second show of Marion Richardson's children's drawings. The exhibition was not a success, but this was only one of Roger's many problems. Edward Wolfe, who in recent months had been the only promising artist working with him, succumbed to influenza and had to go abroad to recuperate. Roger could no longer get furniture made for decoration and had to search for second-hand pieces. In February he wrote to Vanessa of the exhibition:

. . . I'm simply tired out with all the cares of the Omega . . . Then when Wolfe got ill I had to do everything – all the furniture painting. I have surpassed myself in ingenuity inventing methods for treating this old and rough furniture without the long processes of getting a good surface, and also in designing things which could be carried out on the old rough paint, using where possible the original design or what was left of it. On an average, I think I must have designed and painted one piece of furniture per day and some I would love to show you because I think they're the best things we've done in that direction.

It's a really good show – with a lot of wonderful things arranged all round the walls of the big room pinned on to Holland curtains. They produce a very good effect because they are so solid and definite in colour and design. Then I have a lot of Larionov's wonderful designs for marionettes in the studio and then the downstairs room emptied of all but furniture. They look much better than they've ever done before, especially the back room. But it was a horrible wet day yesterday and no one turned up to the private view. However I induced Clutton Brock [of *The Times*] to come for the children's drawings. Do you know he's got quite idiotic about visual art. Among the children's drawings he picked out all the feeble sentimental ones and missed all that was good. Miss Richardson who had believed in him was bitterly disappointed.[30]

In March he wrote to her again: 'This last show has been an utter fiasco. By being abject for most of an afternoon to Mrs Matthias I have sold two chairs for £4, and that's all.'[30]

Vanessa was tied to Charleston with her new baby, who for the first few months did not gain weight. Nina Hamnett, with whom Roger was having a brief affair, had returned to Paris. Roger himself wanted to travel again after the restrictions of the war, but there was now no one to leave in charge of the Omega. Even if the business could survive a hiatus while Fry went abroad, there was none of the old camaraderie and spirit of fun and improvization for Roger to look forward to on his return. It was obvious that the critics were determined to boycott the Omega exhibitions, and the artists who had once been involved with it no longer really required its patronage. It had long since failed to pay anyone a decent wage. There were hopes that an American lady might buy the Workshops and take them over, but eventually Roger decided it was inevitable that they had to close.

The closing sale of the Omega was held in June 1919, and all the remaining stock was sold at half-price. The sale was a success as friends happily bought up the goods on offer: David Garnett bought several tables cheaply for a bookshop that he was planning to set up. In October Roger left for three months of travel and painting in Provence, where he visited Cézanne's home near Aix. In November Virginia wrote to him:

> It may be fancy, but the whole neighbourhood of Fitzroy Square sounds a little dull and hollow, when that enormous vibration – your presence – is removed. You know one can hear it a mile off. I was conscious of this when I went to the private view at Heal's the other day . . .[32]

The Omega had served its purpose in solving the immediate problems of the young artists who, in 1913, were experimenting with Post-Impressionism. Its products introduced a new taste, which was subsequently exploited by fabric and rug designers and showed that England did not entirely ignore movements in decorative arts that were taking place in Europe. Roger had greatly enjoyed his involvement with pottery, and Duncan and Vanessa were to continue exploring the possibilities of interior decoration. Where the Omega had significantly failed was in Roger's vision of forming a group of artists who would inspire one another and force out new ideas. Although opinions had changed drastically since 1910 when Roger had outraged society by his Manet exhibition, the Omega undoubtedly suffered from continuing personal antagonism from the critics. Perhaps if Duncan, and thus Vanessa, had been able to remain in London, the outcome of the Omega would have been different, for Duncan had enjoyed his work there and Roger admired his style greatly. But the Omega remained true to its ideal of spontaneous improvization and Edward Wolfe remembers the atmosphere there as full of fun and creativity.

In her biography of Roger Fry, Virginia Woolf summed up the ending:

> So the Omega workshops closed down. The shades of the Post-Impressionists have gone to join the other shades; no trace of them is now to be seen in Fitzroy Square. The giant ladies have been dismounted from the doorway and the rooms have other occupants. But some of the things he made still remain – a painted table; a witty chair; a dinner service; a bowl or two of that turquoise blue that the man from the British Museum so much admired. And if by chance one of those broad deep plates is broken, or an accident befalls a blue dish, all the shops in London may be searched in vain for its fellow.[33]

5

New departures

AT the beginning of 1919 Duncan took a studio in London at 18 Fitzroy Street. Vanessa, though she took over the lease of a friend's flat at 36 Regent Square, spent most of the spring at Charleston. With the war over, Duncan was free to help her with the decoration of the house and once again the disorganized household provided Virginia with fodder for letters to friends while she was at Asheham:

> But what is one to do with Nessa and Duncan? We all wear clothes; why should they be allowed to go about naked? That's how it strikes me . . . We're going for a picnic today, as it's Nessa's birthday – I'm terrified to think which, but it doesn't seem to matter much.[1] [Vanessa was forty on 30 May 1919.]

> Nessa presides over the most astonishing menage; Belgian hares, governesses, children, gardeners, hens, ducks, and painting all the time, till every inch of the house is a different colour.[2]

Not everyone was convinced of the attractions of Duncan and Vanessa's decorative schemes. Virginia teasingly told Vanessa that she had felt compelled to warn some friends – the Richmonds – who had enquired about renting Charleston:

> And they wanted to know if you'd ever let them Charleston; upon which I said 'Well, Vanessa's ideas of decoration –' but I couldn't go on. 'Yes?' said Elena. 'She's done most of it herself – stuck up bits of paper, you know' – Here came one of the horrid pauses. 'I'm sure she must have made it look very nice' Elena said kindly; but Bruce, who's got some sort of wits about him, was *not* sure.[3]

At the end of the summer Vanessa settled in Regent Square. But the flat was small and she had no cook, and she soon found herself disenchanted with city life, having been away from it for three years. The flat was not close enough to Duncan's studio in Fitzroy Square for her to visit him easily, and she was tied down by the children's meals and school home-work, which left her too tired to see her friends. London seemed busier than it had been before the war; she did not have enough space to paint anything big; and she yearned for the old easy state of things. Roger, in France, wrote constant letters full of the news of Paris and Provence, with plans to found a colony of painters where they could enjoy the Mediter-ranean light and heat. In October Clive left for Paris and Vanessa began to consider seriously Roger's plans to live in freedom abroad.

November brought a few lighter moments. Vanessa went to see the Picasso/Cocteau ballet *Parade* and an exhibition of Matisse's work at the Leicester Gallery, and was glad of a visit from Roger's friend, the poet Charles Vildrac. But in December Julian and Quentin caught influenza and were in bed, so that she could not paint. She was now tantalized not only by Roger's happy letters but also by Clive's ecstatic accounts of his success in Paris and his plans to find a studio there for Duncan and herself:

> Meanwhile my life here is so fantastically successful that I blush to tell of it . . . The Nouvelle Revue and Le Temps have asked me to write for them. Gide says the translation of my book will be an 'évènement litéraire et artistique'. I am invited to lunch and dine every day; and, naturally, I enjoy myself. Bloomsbury is altogether to the fore – the name of Grant is pronounced with respect amongst the artists, that of Keynes amongst the intellectuals, that of Lytton Strachey amongst the littré, unluckily as much and more must be said for the names of Chesterton, Wells and Butler. Fry is slightly demodé – don't repeat this.[4]

> . . . I am a great success here. The explanation is very simple: in a foreign country one belongs to no set and has no enemies 'on principle' – consequently one need only be amiable. A slight reputation preceded me, and it was naturally assumed that if I took the trouble to follow it, it was to make myself neither a nuisance nor a bore. Duncan has more friends here than he supposes. Everyone who saw 'Twelfth Night' remembers it with pleasure; and I have got it firmly into the heads of the French artists that he is the interesting man in England – how furious the others will be when they find out.[5]

Then in April 1920 Vanessa's turn came, and she set off for Rome with Duncan and Maynard. She was immediately in her element. Her delight in freedom after the war years, with all their anxieties and privations, was recorded, as usual, in a letter to Roger:

> We have been trying to paint in gouache but without much success I think. Are you a master of it? It seems to be very difficult not to get it rather leaden

and cold in colour – in fact we are more or less falling back upon water colour
. . . Perhaps you would think it absurd to come to Rome and paint still lives
in a studio – but that is what we have both been doing. But you know even in
a studio the colour is quite different from England . . . The Roman colour is
unlike any other isn't it – one gets to like the place more and more. After 6 years
of England I often find it almost incredible that here one is in Italy again. I think
it will all vanish suddenly and I shall find myself at Charleston or Gordon Sq.
One had got to think it impossible the war would ever come to an end or that
we would ever get abroad again and even now I don't quite know how I *have*
managed to dispose of my children and all and come away. We are shopping
wildly and extravagantly, egged on by Maynard's calculations as to the true
value of the lira . . . frames . . . furniture . . . pottery . . . I hope we shall stop
at various places on our way north and perhaps shall find some modern peasant
pottery there.[6]

On their way north they stopped, at Maynard's insistence, at Bernard
Berenson's villa, I Tatti, outside Florence, although both Duncan and
Vanessa found it difficult to relax in that epicurean household. They also
stopped in Paris and visited Picasso, whose company they found more
sympathetic.

Vanessa's discontent with London never disappeared, especially during
the gloomy winter months. In December 1921 Virginia reported that

Nessa is as usual uncertain what to do – whether to plant the children at
Gordon Square and stay on with Duncan in France, or to face family life in
London. She seems more than ever contemptuous of England – What a bore
it must be to be a painter, and need light and landscape, instead of a fire and a
book![7]

The following year Vanessa took rooms again at 46 Gordon Square,
where Clive was still living. London was the centre for Duncan and
Vanessa's work. They enjoyed the theatre, the exhibitions and the
stimulation of their established and growing circle of friends. But whereas
Duncan enjoyed the social whirl and the slightly outrageous goings-on,
Vanessa could, on occasion, disdain it all, and found some of the younger
generation intolerable. Virginia described her demeanour at a party given
by Karin Stephen:

Vanessa, who had not dressed, sat commandingly on a sofa, talking to a
sculptor called Tomlin, and no one else, for she is beyond the pale now, makes
no attempt to conciliate society, and often shocks me by her complete indifference to all my floating loves and jealousies, but with such a life, packed

like a cabinet of drawers, Duncan, children, painting, Roger – how can she budge an inch or find a cranny of room for anyone?[8]

During the 1920s Vanessa and Duncan divided their time in England between London and Charleston, with annual visits to Europe, often to Paris. There they could catch up on the work of the painters they admired, especially Picasso, Matisse and Derain, and could paint in an atmosphere congenial to them. For the group of 'Bloomsbury' friends the years after the war saw the consolidation of their successes. Virginia, especially, blossomed with three highly praised novels published between 1925 and 1928. If any of the group went unrecognized it was the artists.

The furore of Post-Impressionism had been forgotten and the public found new styles to misunderstand and execrate. With the ending of the Omega in 1919, Vanessa and Duncan no longer belonged to a recognized group of artists, and together they went their own way stylistically, paying little attention in their work to contemporary English movements. Even Roger, who had by now received the respectability of the elder statesman of art criticism, was essentially out of tune with the latest developments in art, especially abstraction.

England itself was falling further behind the French vanguard of painting and decorative arts, and commentators were indecisive about which styles to support. This led, however, to a healthy eclecticism in their acceptance of differing idioms. There were no longer any set rules, making it possible for Duncan and Vanessa' idiosyncratic style to find a market. They never worked as commercial interior decorators, but during the 1920s undertook several commissions for the houses of family and friends. Vanessa always stressed the need to disguise the drabness of London life and was happy to cheer up a friend's flat; in some cases the original suggestion to do so came from herself or Duncan.

In the early 1920s Europe presented two definite lines of thought in design. One, stemming from the Bauhaus in Germany, was little known in England and probably unappealing because of its origins in what had until recently been enemy territory. Its theories did not really begin to seep into England until the 1930s. The other was Art Deco, which culminated in the Exposition des Arts Décoratifs (from which the term itself was later derived) held in Paris in 1925. The work of the French designers varied from the Neo-classical splendour of Emile-Jacques Ruhlmann and Süe et Mare to the rational work of Le Corbusier, shown in the Pavillon de l'Esprit Nouveau, from the designs of Pierre Legrain and Eileen Gray, inspired by Cubism and African art, to the colourful avant-garde decorations of Robert and Sonia Delaunay, or the rich use of lacquer by Jean Dunand. All, however, showed a luxury and sophistication which were disdained by the British, who chose to exhibit the plain, homely woodwork of Ambrose Heal and Gordon Russell. *The Architectural Review* summed up the French contributions:

> Unquestionably every Englishman who visits the pavilions and stands of the modern French *ensembliers* will ask himself whether he would care to live among such impeccable surroundings from which cosiness is markedly absent . . . But little doubt that our Englishman, mindful of fireside joys, of capacious easy chairs, will, perhaps admire, then turn aside and leave such artificialities to the exhibition and to France.[9]

The 1925 exhibition also showed a variety of work from other countries, including the Constructivists in the Russian pavilion, Gio Ponti in the Italian and Georg Jensen in the Danish, which only served further to highlight England's conservatism.

The vital element which did emerge in England as a result of the bewildering array of styles available was the importance of the interior decorator. There was a strong revival of Regency styles, well suited to refurnishing London's housing stock, and many designers played with this theme in their own ways. The best known was Syrie Maugham, who made her name as a decorator at this time. She pioneered the 'all-white' look, with fine period furniture, mirrored screens and rugs by Marion Dorn – though in pre-smokeless London this vogue did not last long.

Before the end of the war Duncan and Vanessa had already begun on a scheme of decoration for Maynard Keynes's sitting-room at Gordon Square, and they also executed new panels for his rooms in Cambridge, completed in 1922. That year they decorated rooms in London for Adrian and Karin Stephen, in 1924 for Virginia and Leonard and in 1926 for Clive. Among their friends they carried out a third scheme for Clive's mistress Mary Hutchinson, when she and her husband moved to Regent's Park in 1926. They decorated rooms for Angus Davidson (brother of the painter Douglas Davidson), who worked at the Hogarth Press; L. A. Harrison, a painter of Walter Sickert's generation; the critic Raymond Mortimer, whom they met through Clive; Ethel Sands, who had previously employed them through the Omega; and the poet Lady Dorothy Wellesley, who was a friend of Virginia's (see Chapter 6).[10]

Contemporary publications, such as *The Studio* or *The Architectural Review*, illustrated their work along with apparently opposing and clashing theories of design. An example of this comfortable jostling of attitudes was Dorothy Todd and Raymond Mortimer's 1929 book *The New Interior Decoration*, in which Duncan and Vanessa were given equal prominence with Le Corbusier, Mies van der Rohe, Marion Dorn and McKnight Kauffer, leaving the reader to wonder what the coherence of style suggested by the title could possibly be.

Vanessa and Duncan's decorative schemes of the 1920s showed a complete break with the house style of the Omega. The bizarre animals, abstract swimming figures and stylized dancers of Duncan's earlier decorations gave way to a much gentler, more lyrical vocabulary. Where figures were used they tended to be variations on characters from classical myths, some of which can be identified (Narcissus and Echo, Daphne and Apollo, Psyche and Cupid, Arion, Europa, Pomona), but which were mainly 'slyly allusive', as Raymond Mortimer put it, and corresponded to a wider appreciation of the historical and artistic interpretations of such legends. Duncan's decorative vocabulary was echoed by the version of Greek paganism which their friend E. M. Forster found in Italy and expressed in his novels and short stories. Forster felt that in Italy the spirits of love and nature could respond to the call of the wild without the harsh elements of Greek *hubris*, but that the cold climate of England suppressed this wilful and joyful paganism. Duncan's figures often illustrate the lyrical voluptuousness of such a mythology. His figures were now fully rounded and solid, expanding to fill the space available, but with an amplitude completely foreign to the compressed energy of his Omega designs. The ultimate success of the decorative commissions lay in the large mural and dado panels, which were generally executed either at Charleston or abroad and taken to their destination to be put in place when finished. The subject-matter of these 1920s commissions shows an obvious affinity with the decorative treatment of Italian interiors and furniture, such as *pietra dura*, gilded mouldings or murals. A bowl of fruit, fans, shells and flowers, a round-bodied white vase full of red tulips and lilies with startling yellow stamens, books, musical instruments, a woman playing the mandolin, all recur frequently in their work and, again, abundantly fill the space allotted. Possibly the earliest examples of the vases of arching flowers are those on the doors which Vanessa painted in Duncan's bedroom at Charleston in 1916.

The preoccupation with mass and density which Roger advocated disappeared in favour of purely decorative devices, which Raymond Mortimer referred to as Vanessa and Duncan's distinctive calligraphy. Borders of continued criss-cross, rows of dots within circles, vertical columns of circles connected by parallel lines suggesting grooved pillars, or small squares alternating with circles, were used to decorate fireplaces and mantelpieces, to outline doors or as borders for rectangular or arched panels filled in with simple, dabbed-on colour, achieving a moiré or stippled effect similar to that described by Roger in *Colour* magazine in 1917. There was no attempt at exact uniformity or a smooth finish, and it is precisely this vivacity of movement, the obviousness of the brushwork, which gives the impression of calligraphy and enlivens the schemes. These devices were repeated on walls, doors, tiles, bookcases and lampshades.

Where these effects scored was in the use of colour. The bold reds, yellows, greens and blacks of the Omega period were abandoned for gentler pastel shades in keeping with contemporary fashion. Duncan and Vanessa used the same colours as in their paintings and constantly demonstrated the ease and confidence of the experienced artist rather than the mind of the decorator. The choice of the base colour, for example, was extremely important, or the use of a completely different tone to suggest shadow instead of merely a darker shade of the same colour.

Vanessa and Duncan did not limit their decorative work to specific commissions. During the 1920s they also designed book jackets, needlework, tiles, theatre sets and costumes, pottery and carpets. Virginia and Leonard had started the Hogarth Press in 1917, and Vanessa designed the jackets for all her sister's books as well as occasionally providing woodcut illustrations. Duncan also did some book jackets for the Hogarth Press, besides creating designs for friends, such as catalogue covers for the bookshop which David Garnett started with Francis Birrell in 1921, or for *Fanfare*, a magazine edited by Leigh Henry, which ran for a few months in 1922. Most of Duncan's designs for book jackets or illustrations, however, date from after the Second World War. Vanessa's and Duncan's designs seldom ventured far from their familiar idioms, and possibly what began as 'doodling' or sketching often proved to be the basis of a scheme for tiles or needlework. The success of their interiors was a result of the uniformity of effect which they achieved because they were responsible for everything, often blending period furniture with the decorations by designing chair covers and ornamenting fireplaces with their own tiles.

Jackets by Vanessa Bell for two of Virginia Woolf's books. 'Walter Sickert' was published by the Hogarth Press in 1934, 'Between the Acts' in 1941.

At the Omega, Vanessa had worked Duncan's designs for needlepoint embroidery. They now both designed chair covers, mirror frames and decorative panels which they persuaded their friends and acquaintances to execute for them. Vanessa would sometimes give Virginia cushion designs to work; and Duncan's mother, Mrs Ethel Grant, seemed an obvious choice as an embroidress. She was not very keen at first, but in the early 1920s she consulted Dr Emile Coué in Nancy, who was famed for his success in auto-suggestion, and with his help persuaded herself that she would enjoy the work. (It was Dr Coué who advised his clients to say to themselves, 'Every day, in every way, I am getting better and better.') Many of the best embroideries were worked by Ethel Grant. In his notes for a paper read to the Lewes Art Society, Duncan wrote:

As you will see these designs are not extremely perfectly drawn out on the canvas and the colours are merely suggested. These she learned in time to *interpret* with considerable success. Her eye for colour combinations became trained to the extent, that having to choose among a variety of wools, she rarely chose a colour which was not harmonious. . . . She said she was an artist, which I thought was true.[11]

In October 1925 designs by Vanessa, Duncan and Roger were included in the exhibition Modern Designs in Needlework at the Independent Gallery in London, organized by the painter Mary Hogarth. The rug designer Ronald Grierson got to know Mary Hogarth in the early 1930s and remembered her as

> a great personality. She was quite elderly and wore her grey hair in long ringlets and wore a crinoline. Her voice was a deep contralto . . . When she came to see me she wore a Victorian poke bonnet. I have never seen anyone like her before or since. Although very downright in her ideas she was kindness itself to me and her work was beautiful.[12]

She executed many designs for Duncan and Vanessa and was subsequently elected by their friends at *Vogue* to that magazine's 'Hall of Fame'.

Vanessa often gave painted tiles as presents to friends; Beatrice Mayor, Margaret Bulley, Ethel Grant, the painter Edward Le Bas, and Leonard and Virginia were among the many who owned tiled tables. Duncan and Vanessa used to go to Greenwich where a Mr James allowed them to decorate the tiles he made and fired. The tables were made up by Kallenborns, who had made furniture for the Omega. In 1929 Vanessa and Duncan began selling their tables through the London Artists' Association.

Following his earlier collaboration with Jacques Copeau, Duncan continued his interest in theatre design. In 1914 two new dancers, Lydia Lopokova and Léonide Massine, had come to London with the Ballets Russes. They were quickly drawn into the parties given at Gordon Square, and in 1925 Maynard Keynes married Lopokova. Duncan designed sets and costumes for three ballets in which she danced: *Togo, or, The Noble Savage* in 1923, the divertissements at the Coliseum in 1924, and *The Postman* in 1925. At this time he also designed the decor and costumes for Beatrice Mayor's play *The Pleasure Garden* and Lytton Strachey's *Son of Heaven*.

Through Maynard and Lydia Keynes, Duncan and Vanessa were involved in a rather select club, the Carmargo Society, which was started to promote interest in ballet in London. Keynes became its treasurer in 1931, Frederick Ashton its director, Lopokova danced, William Walton wrote music, Osbert and Edith Sitwell supplied texts and John Armstrong, Augustus John, Duncan and Vanessa designed the decors. The Carmargo held its first production in October 1930 and staged about three ballets a year for two years, providing a bridge between Diaghilev's death in 1929 and the emergence of the Sadler's Wells Ballet. In 1934 the Carmargo donated its assets and profits to the Vic-Wells Ballet.

In 1931 Duncan designed the sets and costumes for *The Enchanted Grove*, choreographed by the young dancer Rupert Doone, whose portrait Duncan painted. In the following year he provided the sets and costumes for Act II of *Swan Lake*, based on ideas from Inigo Jones, and Vanessa supplied designs for *High Yellow*, choreographed by Ashton. Sir Frederick Ashton remembers these designs as being immensely effective and full of colour in their evocation of a South Sea island; he also recalls Vanessa's sense of humour and the ease with which both she and Duncan collaborated with the others involved in the Carmargo Society productions. In 1933 Vanessa again designed sets and costumes for a Sadler's Wells ballet by Ashton, *Pomona*. In 1934 she provided the decor for *Fête Galante*.

Vanessa and Duncan had by now successfully established a partnership which was to last for almost fifty years. They were still developing together and had not reached a period when their cross-influences were fully worked out – if, indeed, they ever felt they were. Most people, in discussing their work, have tended to assume that Duncan's was the stronger influence, probably because he remained the better known of the two. Raymond Mortimer, who knew them both well, wrote in 1944:

> It is sometimes assumed that she is, as it were, his pupil. Certainly there are conspicuous similarities between Vanessa Bell's work and Duncan Grant's, and often they have painted from the same model. Yet it seems to me clear that the influence has not been one-sided but reciprocal. Careful comparison suggests moreover, that, though they share many tastes, they are quite unlike in temperament. Vanessa Bell is, I think, by nature a realist. (Unlike Grant she has a great gift for catching a likeness.) She is altogether a graver, less exuberant, artist; her landscapes and still-lifes bear the signs of careful consideration and are all the better for this . . . The tempo natural to her is andante while his is allegro.[13]

In artistic terms one may regret the influence of Duncan on Vanessa's work, for there is ample indication that she was the stronger painter. The intensity and force of her early work, the urgent desire to push through the strength of a familiar image, were seldom present in Duncan's more relaxed *flâneur* vision. But Vanessa was influenced by his lightness of touch into partly abandoning her more serious and considered stance and she lost much of the compelling gravity of her early work, or at least failed to develop it satisfactorily in her later paintings. But on a personal level, Duncan's character exercised a beneficial influence.

36 *Mary Hutchinson's drawing room at 3 Albert Gate, Regent's Park, London, decorated by Duncan Grant and Vanessa Bell between 1926 and 1928.*

37 *Clive Bell's library at 50 Gordon Square, London, decorated by Duncan Grant and Vanessa Bell in 1926–27.*

38, 39   Two views of
Lady Dorothy
Wellesley's dining
room at Penns-in-the-
Rocks, Sussex,
decorated by Duncan
Grant and Vanessa
Bell between 1928 and
1930.

40, 41   Two views of
the Music Room
exhibited by Duncan
Grant and Vanessa
Bell at the Lefevre
Gallery, London, in
1932–33.

42 'The Little Urn',
*printed linen by
Duncan Grant,
1933–34.*

43 'The West Wind',
*printed cotton by
Duncan Grant, 1931.*

44   *Printed lin
Vanessa Bell, c*

45   Plates designed by Angelica Bell for Foley China, 1935.

47, 48   Plates designed by Duncan Grant (above) and Vanessa Bell (below) for Clarice Cliff, 1932–34.

46   Plate made by Quentin Bell at Wedgwood in 1936 from an original Omega mould by Roger Fry.

49　Dinner service decorated by Vanessa Bell and Duncan Grant on Wedgwood blanks, commissioned by Kenneth Clark in 1932. The images at the lower right are 'Miss 1933', Duncan, Vanessa, and Greta Garbo.

◁ 50 Teapot made and
decorated by Quentin Bell,
bearing his initial
intertwined with that of his
wife, Olivier.

51 Two pots thrown and
decorated by Quentin Bell.

52 Vase cast by Phyllis
Keyes from an original
brought back from Tunis by
Duncan Grant in 1914,
painted by Duncan. An
almost identical vase was
exhibited in the Music
Room in 1932–33 (see ill.
41).

53 Bowl with lid thrown
by Quentin Bell and
decorated by Duncan Grant.

△ 54   *Painted tiled stove
by Duncan Grant,
commissioned in 1925 by
Miss Margaret Bulley
who lived in Gordon
Square, London.*

55   *Carpet design by
Duncan Grant for the
Queen Mary, 1936.*

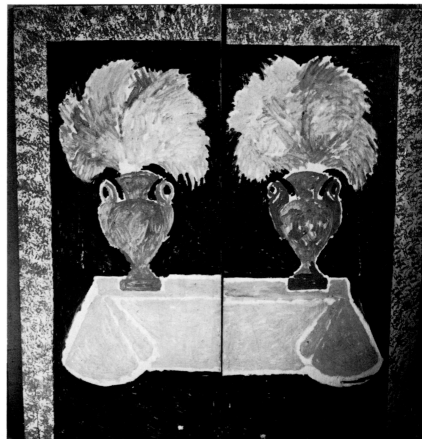

56   *Painted firescreen at
Charleston.*

KEW GARDENS
BY
VIRGINIA WOOLF

DECORATIONS
BY
VANESSA BELL
THE
HOGARTH PRESS

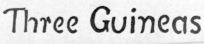

Three Guineas

Virginia Woolf

the Waves
Virginia Woolf

THE DEATH of THE MOTH

VIRGINIA WOOLF

57–62   Book jackets designed by Vanessa Bell for Hogarth Press editions of Virginia Woolf's work: Kew Gardens *(1919),* The Waves *(1931),* Three Guineas *(1938),* The Death of the Moth *(1942),* A Haunted House and Other Stories *(1943), and* Granite and Rainbow *(1958).*

Vanessa designed the jackets for all her sister's books published by the Hogarth Press, as well as for Henry Green's Back *(1946), and* Olivia *by 'Olivia' – Dorothy Strachey, the wife of Simon Bussy (1949). Duncan Grant designed the jacket for Julia Strachey's* Cheerful Weather for the Wedding, *published by the Hogarth Press in 1932.*

63 *The white jug which appeared in so many of Duncan Grant's and Vanessa Bell's paintings and designs (see below), photographed in the garden at Charleston.*

64 *Firescreen at Monks House commissioned by Virginia Woolf c.1924–28, worked by Ethel Grant to a design by Duncan featuring the white jug.*

65　*The dining room at Monks House, with table and chairs designed and painted by Duncan Grant and Vanessa Bell. On the chair backs are Virginia's initials.*

66   Some pots on the window sill at Monks House. Left to right: a
small jug cast by Phyllis Keyes, a jug decorated by Angelica Bell,
and a cup and bowl thrown by Quentin Bell.

6

The thirties

I N 1921 Virginia adroitly observed the essential passivity in Duncan's nature; a letter from Vanessa having taken a week to arrive, Virginia gave her own explanation:

> With Duncan in the house, though, I suppose one can't count upon getting letters posted. Why don't you turn out his pockets on Fridays? Why don't he write to me? He reminds me rather of the Lemur ape, who as you know gets all the other apes to feed it because it is too lazy to feed itself, and also too beautiful.[1]

Duncan had a natural independence which created ease in his relationship with Vanessa. She organized the household and family, and he lived happily within it, content to defer to her feelings and opinions. His casual, happy-go-lucky attitude to life absolved him from any pressures of responsibility she might feel. The inherent seriousness of their relationship lay in their closeness as painters. They both cared deeply about their work and it was there, rather than as lovers, that they met and bonded. Their partnership was complex, but extremely happy.

Clive and Roger visited Charleston constantly. Vanessa and Clive both lived in Gordon Square in London and Vanessa would still go with him at Christmas to visit his parents in Wiltshire. Quentin Bell has written of his father arriving at Charleston with riches in the form of chocolate, usually accompanied by his beautiful and well-dressed mistress of the moment. Both Vanessa and Virginia were called upon to sympathize with his romantic problems or, when he began to develop a bald patch, his fear of growing old. Roger was devoted to Vanessa's children and greatly appreciated the peace and homeliness of Charleston. In 1925 he wrote that he considered it the most peaceful domestic existence conceivable; there's only Clive, Vanessa and the children. It might be held up as a model of what family life ought to be. The extraordinary thing is that the two boys amuse themselves wildly with almost nothing particular to do. Quentin is always happy where there's mud and water. They spend the whole evening concocting the News Bulletin which appears at breakfast the next morning generally typewritten. It contains a fantastic version of the daily events, generally much to Vanessa's discredit – a good many satirical and comic poems illustrated by Quentin, and a weather prophecy . . . Angelica is imperious and irresistible and every afternoon after tea I am set to work to make toys out of corks, cardboard, wire and such like with a good many contradictory instructions as the work progresses, so that it was something of a miracle that a kind of merry-go-round with flying birds on the end of strings did finally emerge.[2]

Virginia continued to enjoy Vanessa's muddled lifestyle, although there were occasional tensions. After a bout of flu she wrote to Vanessa, who had recently taken a studio in Paris for a month with Duncan:

Yes, I was rather depressed when you saw me – What it comes to is this: you say 'I do think you lead a dull respectable absurd life – lots of money, no children, everything so settled: and conventional. Look at me now – only sixpence a year – lovers – Paris – life – love – art – excitement – God! I must be off.' This leaves me in tears.[3]

Virginia often admitted her jealousy of Vanessa's motherhood, especially as it was managed amid so many activities, but she made up for her childlessness through her closeness to her nephews and niece. She was devoted to Angelica, visited her when she went to boarding school, gave her a regular dress allowance and joined enthusiastically in her birthday celebrations. When Angelica was eleven, Virginia went to her 'Alice in Wonderland' party dressed as the March Hare, with Leonard as the Carpenter, but Roger had already stolen the show as the White Knight. She also used to visit Quentin at school, took care when she wrote to him as he couldn't decipher her handwriting, and together they regularly concocted satirical and scandalous accounts of their friends' activities. She later advised Julian on the poetry he wrote at Cambridge. Virginia, indeed, felt it her duty to add some degree of literacy to the children's lives and they fully responded to her wit and kindness.

Virginia's generosity did not stop with Vanessa's children. When Vanessa's ageing car needed further repairs, Virginia offered £100 for a new car as a joint birthday present to her and Duncan. Many escapades were planned with the Charleston household, especially charades and plays, such as a production of *Freshwater*, based on their eccentric great-aunt, the photographer Julia Margaret Cameron; this was planned for Christmas 1923, but Virginia did not complete it until 1935.

Vanessa once remarked that, when they were quite young children, Virginia asked her which parent she liked better. Vanessa preferred her mother, Virginia her father. Virginia was always aware of the problems of entering the male domain of professional work while retaining a feminine insight in her writing, and sought a sexual neutrality among her fellow writers. Vanessa had broken many of the accepted rules of her society in order to achieve a lifestyle which could include both her desire to paint and the happy domesticity she enjoyed. She had her own high and stern standards for her work, but cared little for the business of allocating positions or seeking recognition. Within her relationships her femininity was always stressed and Virginia admired her greatly for her life 'packed like a cabinet of drawers'.

In December 1926 Vanessa and Duncan went for the first time to Cassis, a small town just east of Marseilles on the Mediterranean coast of France where many other English artists used to winter. Vanessa soon began looking for a house to buy. She wrote to Virginia in February:

> Painting is a different thing here from what it can be in the winter in England. It's never dark, even when the sky is grey. The light in the . . . studio is perfect and even now one could often work out of doors if one wanted to. It makes so much difference to be sure one won't suddenly be held up in the middle of something by fog or darkness. Also the beauty is a constant delight. The people are very friendly and helpful and living is very cheap . . . it seems more and more ridiculous for painters to spend half their lives in the dark.[4]

Before Duncan and Vanessa left in May they had arranged to rebuild a ruin on the land of an English vine-grower, Colonel Teed. They called the house La Bergère and over the next decade spent periods of several months there almost every year, often visited by their friends.

In March Virginia and Leonard had visited them in Cassis en route to Rome and Sicily, and Virginia wrote home to her friend Vita Sackville-West from Corsica:

> I am writing, with difficulty, on a balcony in the shade. Everything is divided into brilliant yellow and ink black. Clive is seated at a rickety table writing on huge sheets of foolscap, which he picks out from time to time in red ink. This is The History of Civilisation. He has by him Chamber's Dictionary of the

English Language. We all sit in complete silence. Underneath, on the next balcony, Vanessa and Duncan are painting the loveliest pictures of rolls of bread, oranges, wine bottles. In the garden, which is sprinkled with saucers of daisies, red and white, and pansies, the gardener is hoeing the completely dry earth. There is also the Mediterranean – and some bare bald grey mountains, which I look at, roasting in the sun.[5]

From Sicily she wrote to Vanessa: 'Ever since I left Cassis I have thought of you as a bowl of golden water which brims, but never overflows.'[6]

By the end of the 1920s Vanessa had successfully created a way of life in which painting with Duncan blended pleasurably with her ties with family and friends. Although their work was no longer exciting to the critics, they had a secure place within the London art world and could happily pursue their own interests. Their decorative work from this period also reflected their ease and maturity.

In January 1931 Vanessa, Duncan, and another artist, Keith Baynes, lunched with Allan Walton at the Café Royal in London to discuss the possibility of their designing fabrics for him. Walton was six years younger than Duncan. He had studied painting at the Slade, then in Paris, and became a successful interior decorator with a studio in Cheyne Walk. His family owned a bleach and dye works in Collyhurst, Manchester, and his interest in fabrics was a natural result of an artistic training coupled with a knowledge of the trade. In 1925 he designed Marcel Boulestin's first restaurant, in Leicester Square.

In 1931 the first Walton fabrics were exhibited at the Cooling Galleries. Walton, Vanessa, Duncan, Baynes, Frank Dobson, Cedric Morris and Bernard Adeney, all of whom were members of the London Artists' Association, contributed designs. Walton's brother, Roger, took care of most of the practical side of the business in Collyhurst, where the fabrics were screenprinted at the Little Green Dyeworks. They were sold through Walton's shop in the Fulham Road, the Cooling Galleries, Fortnum and Mason's and other interior decorators, such as Curtis Moffat Ltd in Fitzroy Square. In April 1932 more Walton fabrics were exhibited at Zwemmer's bookshop and gallery in Charing Cross Road.

Walton was one of several people exploring the possibilities of artist-designed textiles. Paul Nash had first shown some textile designs in a 1921 Friday Club exhibition in Heal's Mansard Gallery. In 1925 he contributed four designs to Mrs Eric Kennington's fabric printing workshop, 'Footprints', which were sold by Modern Textiles, a shop started by the textile designer Elspeth Ann Little in Beauchamp Place in 1926. In 1929, disillusioned by the difficulties of producing textiles under such limited conditions, Nash took his designs to Cresta Silks Ltd, but soon became dissatisfied when he found machine production equally limiting.

Marion Dorn, an American, had begun producing hand-made batiks in the early 1920s, which she sold through Modern Textiles. In 1930 she abandoned hand production and began supplying several manufacturers with designs for woven and printed fabrics. She is best known, however, for her rugs, woven by Wilton Royal, which earned her the title of 'architect of floors'. In 1934 she founded Marion Dorn Ltd, which supplied many of the leading architects and interior decorators with fabrics and rugs. Vanessa knew Marion Dorn quite well and McKnight Kauffer, with whom she lived, had been a friend of Roger's for many years.

One of the leading textile firms at this time was Edinburgh Weavers, started by Alastair Morton as a branch of his family's firm. He was encouraged in his ideas by refugees from Germany, such as Moholy-Nagy and Naum Gabo. Morton wanted to create modern textiles for the new architecture pioneered by Walter Gropius and Le Corbusier and in October 1937 Edinburgh Weavers introduced their 'Constructivist fabrics', designed by Ben Nicholson, Barbara Hepworth, Ashley Havinden and others. Marion Dorn also supplied the firm with designs. Arts and Crafts ideals lived on in the work of Phyllis Barron, Dorothy Larcher and Enid Marx, all of whom produced their own blocks and hand printed their fabrics. In 1926 an exhibition of Barron and Larcher's work at the Mayor Gallery was favourably reviewed by Roger Fry in *Vogue*.

Vanessa and Duncan's designs for Walton differ greatly from their earlier Omega fabrics. (Indeed, Marion Dorn's designs are closer in spirit to the Omega textiles.) The repeats are on a larger scale, often designed to hang effectively in folds, and the patterns are mostly based on figurative rather than abstract motifs. They are more freely flowing and bolder in conception, showing birds, leaves, clouds, figures or a vase of flowers illuminated by light from a table lamp. The Walton fabrics are pretty and even romantic, and stand in contrast to the more severe patterns used in modernist interiors. Together, Vanessa and Duncan contributed about fifteen designs which, in 1931, ranged in price from 9s. 9d. a yard to 19s. 9d. In 1937 Duncan won a Medal of Merit at the Paris International Exhibition for 'Apollo and Daphne'. Unfortunately Walton's business closed at the outbreak of the Second World War and he died in 1948.

The romanticism shown in their fabric designs was already apparent in the commission Vanessa and Duncan undertook between 1928 and 1932 for Lady Dorothy Wellesley to decorate the dining room at her Sussex house, Penns-in-the-Rocks, near Tunbridge Wells. The house was built in the late seventeenth century and had once belonged to William Penn, the Quaker who founded Pennsylvania. The Wellesleys had a fine collection of Italian Baroque paintings, and Duncan and Vanessa had to adapt their own imagination to the requirements of their client. The decorations in the dining room had a distinct eighteenth-century flavour. Between six large painted panels on the walls were semicircular painted pier tables surmounted by plain rectangles of colour and curved ground glass lights, topped by small octagonal mirrors. Large appliqué sequined curtains and carpets, woven by Wilton Royal, were later added to the scheme. The overall colours were pale grey and grey-green, with other pastel shades of blue-green and petunia; the furniture made to their designs by Kallenborns was also painted. *The Studio* in 1930 reported that 'the general effect is one of iridescence, rather than of any particular colour scheme'. The dining table was octagonal with a central circular motif; the chairs were a curved version of the Omega cane-backed dining chairs, with curving arms and caned sides. The door was picked out with an oval and cyma curve and the six painted panels showed figures cupped within domed recesses, like statuary posed in Adam alcoves.

These paintings were executed at Cassis and showed none of the stiffness of classical statuary. They depicted fluid groups of women and children enacting such themes as 'Bacchanale' and 'Toilet of Venus'. Some were based on early photographs of Julian and Quentin playing at Asheham. The room as a whole demonstrated the artists' desire to enhance and delight. Duncan later said that the room was 'the best thing we did really – wonderful at night with the lights and pictures reflected in the looking-glasses'.[7] The entire scheme cost £775 16s. 7d., of which Duncan and Vanessa received £350.

Following the completion of this commission, Duncan and Vanessa gave an exhibition of their own taste. This was the 'Music Room' shown at the Lefevre Gallery in St James's. The exhibition opened with a party, given by Vanessa and Virginia on 30 November 1932, to which Virginia invited many of her more fashionable friends. Everything was for sale and Virginia had agreed to spend £100 on buying items from the room as a guarantee against possible financial loss. The Music Room was far more exuberant and lively than Penns-in-the-Rocks, using turquoises and yellows rather than quiet pastel shades. Apart from a painted gramophone and baby grand piano, it was more like a comfortable sitting room. Two upholstered chairs and a settee were covered in Duncan's 'Grapes' design, produced by Allan Walton, with matching curtains along the end wall, topped by a specially printed pelmet. There was a large, sophisticated mirror, designed by Vanessa, over a fireplace of decorated tiles, cane-backed chairs with inset ovals of needlepoint, an embroidered duet stool, a painted screen and a painted lamp and lampshade; and six large floral panels, topped with circular mirrors, lined the walls. Two carpets were woven by Wilton Royal and on the mantelpiece stood a pot cast by Phyllis Keyes and decorated by Duncan. The contents of the room demonstrated the artists' versatility and their conviction that anything could be decorated. However, no commissions resulted from the exhibition and Virginia duly bought the mirror, cane chairs, and one of the carpets.

There were several attempts during the 1930s to link artists directly with industry, although generally only in a peripheral manner. In 1933 Brain & Co. of Stoke-on-Trent, who made Foley China, commissioned artists to decorate blanks which could then be used as the basis for mass-produced china. Duncan, Vanessa, and even the fourteen-year-old Angelica, joined Ben Nicholson, Graham Sutherland, Paul Nash, Albert Rutherston and Ernest Proctor as contributors. Duncan's design, 'Old English Rose', was a blown pink rose on a green field, Vanessa's a pattern in yellow and purple with a slight lustre finish, and Angelica's a sort of polka-dot in turquoise, black and red. The Foley China was shown in an exhibition at Harrods called 'Modern Art for the Table': Sir William Rothenstein, who opened the show, commented later, 'So successful were the exhibits that for a time, I was told, they affected the sale of Harrod's usual wares.'[8]

Other china and pottery manufacturers followed suit. Lady Sempill of Dunbar Hay introduced Eric Ravilious to Wedgwood's, who commissioned him to design a coronation range in 1937. In Burslem the Susie Cooper Pottery and Arthur J. Wilkinson & Co., who made Clarice Cliff's 'Bizarre' range, had already discovered the market attraction of a name. Between 1932 and 1934 Wilkinson's enlarged the scope of 'Bizarre' by commissioning well-known artists to contribute to the series. Frank Brangwyn, John Armstrong, Laura Knight, Duncan and Vanessa were all sent blanks to decorate. Laura Knight's circus images were undoubtedly the most successful of the range, which was marketed as a copyright first edition. Tea-sets and dinner services from the 'Bizarre' range were also exhibited in the Harrods show.

Another, more important, area in which artists were increasingly commissioned by industry was advertising and publicity. Frank Pick at London Transport and Jack Beddington at Shell-Mex BP used material by a long list of artists including, for Shell, Vanessa and Duncan.

One of the most long-lived of Vanessa and Duncan's interests was the decoration of ceramics. They had first painted plates at the Omega and Roger had encouraged them to try their hands at throwing, though with little success. For a time, after the Omega closed, they decorated whatever pots came to hand and when abroad they always collected local peasant pottery. During the late 1920s they were introduced to the potter Phyllis Keyes, possibly by the sculptor Stephen Tomlin, who was her assistant for a while. She made casts of Italian and Spanish ceramics which could then be decorated before firing. Although she did some decoration herself, the undoubted draw of the names Grant and Bell must have helped to sell more pots. In 1933 she opened her own kiln and workshop in Warren Street, London, where Duncan and Vanessa would often go; and throughout the 1930s there was a steady working relationship between Miss Keyes and the two artists. As a copyist, her range was quite large, varying from delicate pieces to the large two-handled vase decorated by Duncan and exhibited in the Music Room. This was a copy of a vase he had brought back from Tunis in 1914, and of which he decorated several variations.

The ceramic decorations by Duncan and Vanessa show a distinct casualness, and many of their vases give the appearance of crude and careless execution. But while the shapes of the pots were often awkward, the brush strokes are always definite and controlled, with an attractive lack of diffidence. As artists used to working from a familiar palette, they sometimes had difficulty with colours which would change when fired, but they managed to achieve a bizarre sophistication in their decorations. Their interest in pottery was limited to decoration: they never became involved either in throwing or in glaze techniques. At a time when potters such as Bernard Leach, Michael Cardew and William Staite Murray were becoming influential, this indifference to the medium must have seemed amateurish, yet there is no lack of sympathy towards the clay or the contours of the body.

In 1932 Kenneth Clark commissioned Duncan and Vanessa to decorate a dinner service for him. They produced a vast array of plates painted with portrait heads of famous women, from Marie Antoinette to Charlotte Brontë, from Elizabeth I to 'Miss 1933', and portraits of the two artists, which, although a little insignificant singly, work wonderfully *en masse*, as they were designed to do. They were painted on ordinary glazed white Wedgwood plates and then fired.

In 1936 Quentin Bell went to Stoke-on-Trent to learn about pottery from Thomas Fennemore, who had been Director of Brain & Co. since 1932. Quentin first had a kiln at Charleston in 1936; a new pottery built in September 1939 was hardly used until after the war. He began throwing the local blue clay, but it formed triple silicate of iron at high temperatures and collapsed like glass. Until supplies ran out in the 1940s he used a local red clay from Uckfield which left a warm body colour for decoration. Duncan and Vanessa now had a ready supply of shapes at hand and the whole family decorated pots for display and for household use. Quentin still produces pottery at his home near Charleston:

I very much enjoy decorating pots and I quite enjoy, every now and then, going out and throwing some shapes. I'm bored by any series because I'm not an exact person; I can't make all the cups fit the saucers and that kind of thing. I do think that there are decorative qualities that *only* pottery can give and I always enjoy playing around with new techniques. Recently I've found plates a great stand-by. I like the quality of a thrown plate. For some reason most of my contemporaries don't seem to like making plates, I don't know why it is. In general I do find a mug a comforting and sensible sort of shape to work with and one which allows for an awful lot of playing around with the contour when you're throwing it. But I'll tell you a thing – I wonder if this is usual amongst potters – when one has an idea of what kind of shape one's going to make, the actual determination of the subtler qualities arises in the throwing. It's not a planned or designed thing. It happens as one lifts the clay. I have tried the experiment of putting a mirror into my wheel so that I could follow what I was doing rather more, because it seemed to me altogether too instinctive not to look at the shape that you are making. It's particularly true of a mug or a bowl or a vase. A plate, no. You do see much more clearly what you're doing. But when I did put a mirror in, I found it utterly and completely disconcerting. I have made drawings of shapes I want to make, but on the whole I'd much rather find the shape in the process of making it.

I tend to make things that I'm going to have fun decorating. That's one of the reasons why I make plates such a lot. When I'm throwing a plate I do think, 'Oh, this'll be a lark to decorate' – it'll be a nice field of operations, so to speak. On the whole my tendency of course is just to make whatever is in demand.

Mugs are always in demand. They're functional and therefore people have a good excuse for buying them. Very frequently I make things simply to meet household breakages. Supposing we're out of something, I make it and then of course I make a lot more than I need so then one has a choice.[9]

Against the considered brush marks of Bernard Leach or Shoji Hamada, Quentin's pottery upholds his expressed conviction that there is 'a quite considerable place for vulgarity in life'. His pottery is extremely likeable; it is exuberant and homely, with no refinement or discretion, and bears out Roger's words in the preface to the Omega catalogue: 'The artist is the man who creates not only for need for for joy, and in the long run mankind will not be content without sharing that joy through the possession of real works of art, however humble or unpretentious they may be.'[10]

By the early 1930s England was beginning to establish a more coherent attitude towards design. In 1930 the Society of Industrial Arts was formed. Its members were to include Paul Nash, Frank Dobson, Serge Chermayeff and Ashley Havinden – all names which appear frequently throughout the decade. Three years later the Dorland Hall Exhibition was organized by a group of young architects, Oliver Hill, Wells Coates, Chermayeff and Raymond McGrath, all of whom espoused the modernist ethic of design. Under their generalized lead, various shops and galleries catered for the modern idiom, especially the designer showrooms, such as that of Curtis Moffat, an American married to Iris Tree, whom Duncan and Vanessa had painted in 1915. Moffat used pale colours with modernist rugs and abstract sculpture. Others were Arundell Clarke, who designed the first square upholstered armchair; Denham Maclaren, who used glass, tubular steel and rare woods; Betty Joel, who sold her own rugs and curved veneered furniture; and J. Duncan Miller, who used steel and glass in all-black settings. There were also exclusive outlets, such as Dunbar Hay, run by Lady Cecilia Sempill, which sold Regency Revival furniture and Allan Walton textiles, the new furnishing department at Fortnum and Mason's where Ronald Fleming exhibited furniture by Alvar Aalto, and Chermayeff's Modern Art Studio at Waring & Gillow. When the Bauhaus closed in 1932, several of its designers came to England and their principles were put into production by firms such as Isokon, run by Jack Pritchard.

Against such a determinedly commercial front, there was little room for Duncan and Vanessa's idiosyncratic style of interior decoration. They had never managed to reach much further than their own circle of acquaintances and were now left behind. Their ideas were no longer chic or avant-garde and they had failed to establish themselves on a professional basis during the years when they could have become more generally popular. During this period an incident occurred which demonstrated how far removed they had become from modern styles.

In May 1935 Duncan was commissioned to paint three large panels for the new Cunard transatlantic liner, *Queen Mary*, and also to design and select carpets, curtains and furnishing fabrics. Vanessa was asked by Cunard to provide painted panels and other furnishings for the drawing room. Various artists were commissioned to decorate other parts of the ship. Duncan's three panels were for the overmantel and forward wall of the main lounge. Two measured 11 by $7\frac{1}{2}$ ft (3.35 by 2.30 m) and the third 18 by 13 ft (5.50 by 4 m). Each of the smaller panels, entitled *The Flower Gatherers* and *The Sheaf*, depicted two semi-nude female figures, and the larger one was a group of dancing figures, all in lyrical spring-like settings.

Duncan went to Rome in May, where he began work; he was joined there at the end of the month by Vanessa and Angelica. In September the Cunard architect requested that the scale of the panels be altered and that, since the metal reliefs commissioned from Maurice Lambert as part of the scheme also showed female figures, the number of dancers in the main panel be reduced. A Mr Leach of Cunard wrote to Duncan at this time, 'It is felt that too high a proportion of the murals would appeal only to a limited coterie interested in the development of modern painting, and that this condition must be changed to provide these pictures with wide general appeal.'[11] The changes were agreed and work went on. It was clear from Mr Leach's comment, however, that the Cunard management was already in difficulties over the integration of the artists' work with their overall conception of the liner's decor. That such problems could be avoided was shown in the same year, when the Orient Steam Navigation Company hired the architect Brian O'Rorke to supervise the fittings of their new liner, *Orion*. O'Rorke planned all the decorations in the modern taste, using designers and artists such as Marion Dorn and Ben Nicholson, and the finished *Orion* drew enormous praise.

By February 1936 Duncan gained permission from Cunard to finish his decorations *in situ*. Since September he had been in constant touch with the architects, who had approved his panels and his designs for fabrics and carpets, though at first they had disagreed with his choice of colours.

A few days after the panels had been put in position Sir Percy Bates, the Chairman of Cunard, went aboard to inspect the ship. He immediately rejected Duncan's entire scheme. He agreed to compensate Duncan for his work, but saw no reason to give any explanation for his decision, and the panels remained the property of Cunard.

Duncan's friends – Raymond Mortimer, Kenneth Clark, Samuel Courtauld, Clive Bell, Leonard Woolf and Maynard Keynes – all supported his claim to an explanation of Sir Percy's action. Duncan's primary concern was with the fate of the panels themselves; eventually they were returned to him, with the proviso that he could not exhibit them without Cunard's permission. Sir Percy never gave his reasons for cancelling the commission, but Raymond Mortimer later summed up the probable causes. The panels, he said,

> would have contrasted violently with the style of decoration in which the rest of the ship was lavishly embellished. Moreover, they would certainly not have appealed to the film-stars, opera-singers, oil-magnates and other Big Business tycoons who before the war were bound to be the most valuable patrons of a luxury liner. It would perhaps have been better if the Company had thought of this before commissioning so distinguished and so inappropriate an artist.[12]

At this time the success of the new orders passing through the shipyards, which were just beginning to recover from the depression of the early 1930s, was of vital economic importance, and Sir Percy no doubt acted properly as a businessman. The real issue at stake was voiced by Kenneth Clark at the time:

> With regard to the general question of art in industry, this misadventure should be recorded as showing how little inducement there is for a distinguished artist to take part in any public work. Legally an artist, however distinguished, is no doubt in the same position as an electrical contractor, but if any effort is to be made to employ such men, they must be treated with more consideration.[13]

7

The forgotten years

DUNCAN and Vanessa added constantly to the decorations at Charleston. Whenever they became involved in a new venture the prototypes or, in commercial designs, examples of their work, found their way onto window sills, mantelpieces, walls and chairs. The painted decorations in the house date from 1916, including the doors and fireplace in Duncan's bedroom, the upstairs library, a little log box used in the downstairs sitting room, a bedhead by Duncan showing Morpheus, the God of Sleep, and a linen chest with his favourite 'swimmer' design. In the 1920s a new studio was built on, opening out into the walled garden. From these years date a music stool, embroidered by Ethel Grant for the 1925 Modern Designs in Needlework exhibition, tiled tables, embroidered mirror frames, heavy cylindrical painted lampstands and innumerable pots cast by Phyllis Keyes. In the late 1930s the sitting room and dining room were decorated, the walls of the dining room a dramatic pattern in black, golden-yellow and silver-grey by Duncan, the large circular table by Vanessa, and dining chairs from the Omega. Charleston was never finished, for the possibility of adding to it or trying out new ideas to replace the existing designs was always present.

The most robust account of the household can only be obtained from those who took it for granted. Grace Higgens went to work for Vanessa in May 1920 and remained with the family for almost fifty years, accompanying them to London and to Cassis. When she started work there was no electricity (it was not put in until 1934) and the water was pumped by hand from the pumphouse outside. It was she who cooked, cleaned, and kept the furniture well polished. She obviously never regarded the household as anything particularly out of the ordinary and remembers it with her own sense of priorities:

At breakfast everyone was in the dining room. There would be Clive Bell, and everybody, the visitors too – we just put it in and they helped themselves. And for lunch and dinner, they came out and fetched it. I wouldn't go in because I said I wasn't going in looking grubby, as you are when you're getting things ready. Duncan Grant would come out with a napkin on his arm – I think in his first life he must have been a waiter – or the different ones would help. After breakfast they would sit and have a little chat for a while and then they'd all go to their different parts of the house – Clive Bell would go to his room to write or whatever he was doing, and Duncan to his studio and Mrs Bell to her top studio and Quentin to the pottery, but after he got married of course he wasn't there. And the visitors like Lytton Strachey or Desmond MacCarthy and such like or Roger Fry, they would sit out in the front of the house or in the garden and chat. But Mr Grant would always go to his studio and Mrs Bell to her top studio. In the evenings they all gathered together. That's when they met. You see, they'd have the meals together and chat and then in the evenings the dinner. That was the time that they spent together, chatting and talking. Sometimes Angelica when she was younger would play the piano. Clive Bell always arranged the meats. He would know what he'd like. At Christmas now and again we'd have boar's head, and I remember boar's head struck me as rather marvellous with a lemon in its mouth. He'd get them from Fortnum and Mason's. He liked food very much; he'd have saddles of mutton and pheasants, grouse and jugged hares, and all kinds of things. But Mrs Bell wasn't very interested in food. On her own she would have little meals. Clive Bell was well known as a host in London and he used to entertain Lady Asquith and Princess Bibesco and all those kind of people. But at Charleston the evening was the time when they got together. And then they'd have wine and they'd really enjoy the evening meal; but during the day the meals were just something you had to have. In the beginning they used to have quite a lot of guests. As a matter of fact Angelica said to me the other day when she was on the telephone, 'I can't think where we put them all up. Where did all the guests sleep?' Well, not in each other's rooms – when they went to bed they had their own bed-rooms.

People have blow-ups, don't they – but do you know, all the years I lived there I never heard anything. The only time I ever heard noise was when Mr Bell would yell at the two boys when they were younger. Quentin and Julian were a bit noisy, tearing after cats, or shooting poor cows in the behind with pellets because they were making a noise for the calves. But otherwise they were very quiet. Mrs Bell liked the same kind of things as Mr Grant. He was a happy person. She didn't smile so much, but it didn't mean to say that she was bad-tempered – she was just very quiet, always, to my mind, a Victorian kind of person. Big hat and long dresses – and made them mostly – her hair done in a little chignon thing at the back. Of course when I came to her she must have been 40. She was more serious, but they very much liked the same kind of things. But he was a bit more frivolous-minded, I should imagine. He loved a joke. They both loved Charleston garden, and spent much time in it and painted the flowers taken from it.[1]

Amid all the work, painting and travel of the 1930s, however, there were also sorrows. In January 1932 Lytton Strachey died of cancer, after a long illness. Vanessa had been planning a fancy dress party at her London studio and, hearing that Lytton was in fact a little better, continued with her plans. Then the news came that he had died that afternoon, and Vanessa and Duncan were left to receive their guests in tears. Lytton had been a frequent visitor to Charleston, especially in the early days, and had always remained close to Duncan. Shortly afterwards Carrington, unable to face life without him, committed suicide at Ham Spray, the house she had shared with him since 1924.

In September 1934, soon after returning from a trip to France, Roger fell and broke his thigh. Although in great pain, he seemed to be recovering; but a few days later he died of heart failure. To Vanessa, who was at Charleston, the news came as a grievous blow; the next day she went to London with Virginia and Roger's sister Margery to see Helen Anrep, with whom Roger had been living since 1926 and who had become a close friend of Vanessa's.

In his last few years Roger had been more active than ever with his writings, lectures, painting and travel. In 1933 he had finally achieved the appointment he had long coveted – the Slade Professorship of Fine Art at Cambridge. His death was greatly mourned by all who knew him and Virginia undertook to write his biography – a form of writing which did not come easily to her. But she had prized him highly, as she had written to Vanessa in 1928:

> Roger is the only civilised man I have ever met, and I continue to think him the plume in our cap; the vindication, asseveration – and all the rest of it – If Bloomsbury had produced only Roger, it would be on a par with Athens at its prime (little though this will convey to you). We dined with him, and came away – fed to the lips, but impressed almost to tears by his charm.[2]

Vanessa had lost two of her oldest and closest friends. Then her son Julian was killed in Spain at the age of twenty-nine. In August 1935 he had gone to take the Chair of English at the University of Wuhan in China, supposedly for three years, but at the end of 1936 he wrote home to say that he felt he should be more politically active in the struggle against

Fascism and that he intended to go and fight in Spain for the Republic. He decided to return first to England, where Leonard and Virginia tried hard to persuade him to follow his political convictions in some other way, but in June 1937 he left for Spain. On 13 July there was a pause in the Republican offensive of Brunete and a new plan was under discussion at the Non-Intervention Committee in London. On the 18th the Nationalist forces renewed their attack; one of the casualties of the violent fighting was Julian, who was killed by a bomb while driving an ambulance for the British Medical Unit. When the news reached Vanessa in London on the 30th, she collapsed completely. Virginia and Leonard drove her down to Charleston on 29 July and themselves remained at their Sussex home, Monks House, until October so that Virginia could be near her. Vanessa was confined to bed for several months and later wrote that it was only Virginia's visits which gave her anything to live for. She had felt from the moment Julian left for Spain that she would never see him again, it reminded her of the waste of Thoby's death, for Julian had some of Thoby's confident, idiosyncratic charm and had shown great promise as a writer.

Other friends died during the next few years and the war brought new forms of devastation. Vanessa and Duncan's studios in Fitzroy Street were destroyed by fire; the Woolfs' new house in Mecklenburg Square, and then their former house in Tavistock Square, were both bombed and destroyed. Duncan, Vanessa and Clive moved permanently to Charleston, as did the Woolfs to Monks House. Vanessa gradually became more and more reclusive. Then in 1941 came Virginia's suicide.

In May and June 1940 Duncan had gone to Plymouth as a War Artist: he had refused such a post during the First World War, but felt it was justified in a war opposed to Fascism. In the same year he and Vanessa received a very different commission when the architect Sir Charles Reilly, who lived near Duncan's Aunt Violet in Twickenham and who was familiar with Sussex, suggested to Bishop Bell of Chichester that Duncan do a mural for one of his Sussex churches. Bishop Bell had for long been interested in the association between the Church and the world of art and felt it important that modern artists should be represented in churches to preserve such an association as a living tradition. When he was Dean of Canterbury he had started the annual Festival which included such famous productions as T. S. Eliot's *Murder in the Cathedral* in 1935. During the war, due to the threat of bomb damage, the usual involvement of artists

67 A studio portrait photograph of Vanessa Stephen, probably taken at the time of
her marriage to Clive Bell in 1907, which suggests her beauty and also that
paradoxical combination noticed by Leonard Woolf, between 'tranquillity and
quietude' and, in the depths of her mind, 'an extreme sensitivity, a nervous tension . . .'

69   *Edward Wolfe
and Osbert Sitwell,
c.1918.*

70   *Clive Bell with
Mary Hutchinson.*

71   *a. Roger Fry and Clive Bell at Durbins, c.1913;   b.
Vanessa Bell with Julian and Quentin, possibly at Asheham during
the First World War;   c. Julian Bell, 1920s;   d. Duncan
Grant, Angelica Bell and Roger Fry at Charleston, c.1925;
e. Julian Bell, c.1930;   f. Vanessa Bell at Charleston, c.1920.*

72　*a. Vanessa Bell at Cassis, c.1930;*　　*b. La Bergère, the villa
built by Duncan Grant and Vanessa Bell, Cassis;*　　*c. Duncan
Grant and Vanessa Bell at Cassis, c.1930;*　　*d. On the terrace at
La Bergère;*　　*e. Judith Bagenal (Barbara Bagenal's daughter),
Angus Davidson, Angelica Bell and probably Duncan Grant, at La
Bergère;*　　*f. Angelica Bell and a friend at Cassis, c.1928.*

73   Roger Fry and Duncan Grant
working on a mosaic at Durbins, 1911–12.

75   Angelica Bell in the garden at
Charleston, early 1930s.

74   *Duncan Grant and Quentin Bell at*
Charleston, late 1920s.

76 *Vanessa Bell at work on*
The Annunciation.

79 The Nativity, *by Vanessa*

77, 78 *Chattie Salaman and Vanessa Bell
(left), and Duncan Grant with Angelica
Bell, Quentin Bell and Chattie Salaman,
posing for the murals in Duncan's studio
at Charleston.*

80 *By the window in Duncan Grant's bedroom at Charleston (see also pl. XIV).*

81 *Postcard of Charleston Farm when it was a guest house before the First World War, showing the pond in front of the house. The walled garden is on the right.*

82 *Embroidered cushion in the drawing room at Charleston, designed by Vanessa Bell.*

83   Duncan Grant's studio at
Charleston. The door leads
through to what was Quentin
Bell's pottery.

84   Looking down a corridor to
the studio.

85   *Duncan Grant in his studio at Charleston in April 1977.*

86 *Raymond Mortimer in his drawing room in Islington in 1979.*

87 *Edward Wolfe in his London studio, June 1979.*

88 Grace Higgens outside the Post Office at Firle in 1979. This was the Charleston household's local shop.

89 Barbara Bagenal in her garden at Rye, Sussex, in 1978 with a panel which Vanessa Bell painted for her to hide the gas meters in her London flat.

90 Angelica Garnett in the studio at Charleston in 1979.

91　*Quentin Bell at Cobbe Place, Sussex, in 1979.*

in stained glass was put aside in favour of other schemes, such as mural decoration. Duncan chose the little church of Berwick, around the Downs from Charleston, and proposed that he, Vanessa, Quentin and Angelica collaborate on its decoration. Bishop Bell enthusiastically supported the idea and Maynard Keynes, Kenneth Clark and others helped to finance the scheme.

The proposals were that Duncan should depict Christ in Glory, Vanessa the Annunciation and the Nativity, and Quentin the Parable of the Wise and Foolish Virgins, and that Angelica should work on a decoration for the wall of the south aisle, which was, however, never completed. Work began in 1941 and preparatory sketches were submitted for approval. It seemed best to paint on plasterboard, which could then be put in position in the church, and boards were set up in a large barn beside Charleston where the artists could have the necessary space. However, there was some local opposition to the scheme and an appeal against the murals was submitted to the Chancellor's Court, which met to hear the case in October 1941. Kenneth Clark, Frederick Etchells, who had been appointed official architect for the scheme, T. A. Fennemore of the Society of Mural Painters and others spoke in favour of the plan, and permission was granted by the Court. The paintings were finished in December 1942, installed by January 1943, and were dedicated in a service at the church in October. More decorations were added: Vanessa painted three panels for the pulpit, which were later destroyed by vandals and replaced by Duncan; Quentin added an altarpiece and Duncan decorations to the screen and a large Crucifixion to the west wall.

In 1954 Duncan was approached to submit plans for an ecclesiastical scheme by the Abbey Memorial Trust at Lincoln Cathedral. Vanessa was on the committee of the Edwin Austin Abbey Memorial Trust Fund for Mural Painting in Great Britain and worked with the Dean of Lincoln, Colin Dunlop, on the scheme to decorate the Russell Chantry. At the same time, the arches of the north choir aisle were decorated by Gilbert Spencer, John Armstrong, Clive Gardiner and Louisa Hodgson. The drawings were submitted in January 1956 and by February 1957 the wall paintings were complete, although Duncan's first cartoons had to be revised because of complicated issues concerning the paintings' iconography.

At first sight, it seems strange that so confirmed an agnostic as Vanessa should become involved in schemes to decorate churches. However, both she and Duncan had, from the time of their early travels with Roger had been fascinated by medieval and early Renaissance church paintings, especially the Romanesque frescoes at Saint-Savin-sur-Gartempe in western France, which they visited before the First World War. The chance to experiment with the proportions and scale of a church posed an exciting challenge, particularly since mural commissions were not as plentiful as during the 1920s vogue. The colours of the Berwick interior are on the whole rich and glowing with, in Vanessa's paintings, a vivid use of white areas. The church, however, is quite small and Duncan's figures, especially the *Crucifixion*, appear a little over-large for the space. The most effective decorations are those for the pulpit and screen where the colours are warm, and the *Four Seasons* roundels added by Duncan give a gem-like impression. From the religious point of view, the murals are most successful because of the presentation of modern people and modern dress, showing that the Divine does not need to be represented as archaic. The Berwick church decorations were very much a local affair: Duncan and Vanessa were no longer the national figures they had been before the war.

In 1944 Duncan and Vanessa painted mural decorations for the children's restaurant at the Devonshire Hill School in Tottenham, which was opened by Maynard Keynes in 1946. The paintings, on the theme of Cinderella, have now been destroyed, but people at the school still remember them, one comment being that they looked very old-fashioned – 'more like Queen Victoria and Prince Albert than Cinderella'. In 1951 they did painted tiles for King's College Hostel in Cambridge, and in 1956 Duncan was asked to do the scenery and costumes for John Blow's production of *Venus and Adonis* at the Aldeburgh Festival. The production also went to the Scala Theatre in London with the English Opera Group. Duncan, who was then seventy-one, was delighted with the commission and the opera.

By the end of the war, Duncan, Vanessa and Clive were all in their sixties. Cassis had been given up, and Clive no longer took his long annual visits to Paris. Charleston became their home and their retreat. In 1942 Angelica had married David Garnett and moved to Huntingdonshire. In 1946 Maynard Keynes died at Tilton, the house he had taken, a short walk from Charleston, at the time of his marriage. Duncan and Vanessa missed his practical advice and help, as well as the dimension of a larger political and international life which he had added to their discussions.

Although Duncan and Vanessa lived with many artifacts and decorations from the time of the Omega, to them, obviously, it was merely one part of their lives. But in 1946 Miller's Gallery in Lewes held an exhibition of Omega products, arranged to evoke the interior of 33 Fitzroy Square. Soon afterwards Winifred Gill wrote to Vanessa enquiring about the possibility of there being an Omega room at the Victoria and Albert Museum. Vanessa replied:

> I hope it may happen for I thought the things at Miller's in Lewes looked very good, especially the pottery . . . But one drifts away from people so, even apart from the war – How long ago all that time seems – it was very strange having it revived for a little while by the Miller's exhibition . . .[3]

It must have been unsettling for Duncan and Vanessa to see their work as evocative of an epoch and not merely as one stage in their development as artists. Their past was becoming history.

In 1943 John Rothenstein, the son of Sir William Rothenstein who had attacked Roger's critical views, visited Charleston.

> I found myself in an environment fascinating for its 'period' interest though for other reasons, of course, as well. There were pieces of Omega furniture and carpets and the textiles designed by my hosts, their slightly clumsy yet distinguished pottery embellished by swirls and hooks in their deliberately irregular, their unmistakable calligraphy; also the iron stove, the mustard-coloured wall-paper and other objects made familiar by their pictures. All this and the gentle voices, dying away often, of the artists and the booming voice of the critic [Clive Bell] expressing opinions in which an urbane liberalism blended oddly with unexpected rigidities, strong prejudices more easily sensed than defined. Here I was in the only corner of this vanishing society to survive intact: people and environment, everything: even, out of the windows, could be glimpsed the subjects of so many of the two artists' landscapes.[4]

By the end of the war Charleston was no longer a centre, a gathering place, for English intellectualism: it had become a backwater and, as the years went on, almost an anachronism. When they moved there in 1916 Vanessa had yet to gain the right to vote, the tubular steel chair had yet to be designed . . . there are many comparisons to highlight the sense of time passing. In 1946 they had lived in the house for thirty years, but acrylic paint, jumbo jets, the work of Kitaj or Jasper Johns were still to happen – all things which delighted Duncan when they came to his notice. Vanessa became quieter and liked only the company of people she knew

well. Increasingly, Charleston itself became the subject of her paintings –
a pot on a table, a view of the garden from an upstairs window, a vase of
flowers against a patterned fabric. She closely guarded her territory and
limited her way of life, drawing almost exclusively on the culture of which
she had been a part. Unlike Duncan, whose curiosity was boundless, she
did not welcome insights and inspirations from the world outside.
Vanessa's reclusiveness became a family joke; as Duncan wrote to Clive
during a dreadful winter, after Vanessa's death in 1961, 'We have got into
the local newspaper and said to be completely isolated. But Nessa would
have been delighted as there is no chance of a visitor.'[5]

It is interesting to compare the adjectives which were applied to
Vanessa's and Duncan's work over the years. Vanessa's work was 'ruthless', 'unabashed', 'austere', 'blunt', 'uncompromising' and 'grand'.
Duncan's was 'lyrical', 'witty', 'graceful', 'allusive', 'idyllic' and 'agree-
able'. Vanessa's world had its limits and rules while Duncan's was far
more open and inquisitive, although during her lifetime he was content to
accept most of the limitations which she required for her security. Roger
was probably the love of Vanessa's life, but emotionally she attached
herself to her painting rather than to relationships. In their singleminded
dedication to their work, Duncan and Vanessa were the perfect couple.

Both Charleston and Bloomsbury have been described as Bohemian.
Life at Charleston was, on the surface, casual: activities spilled over into
the garden, the children were free to explore and play as they chose and
there was no dressing for dinner. The household was certainly lax in its
attitudes towards neatness, order and even cleanliness, but such qualities
have little place in a working studio. As new generations visit the house
there is an increasing sense, almost as in a story by Jorge Luis Borges, of
Vanessa and Duncan having 'invented' Charleston; a sense that such an
environment must have been especially created as a backdrop for their
position as 'the only corner of this vanishing society'. It becomes hard to
believe that the reality of the first meetings at Gordon Square could exist
in any form other than published biography and criticism. Their youth
has become so much a part of the received history of the present generation
that it is difficult to detach our knowledge and give it back to those who
really experienced it. So Charleston gives the impression of an invention
conceived as the ratification of published history. It is this almost un-
avoidable, but nevertheless bogus, suggestion of artificiality which prompts
the accusation of a studied bohemianism in their way of life.

Both Vanessa and Duncan lived longer than their reputations, yet Charleston betrays no hint of regret or failure, only the sense that fully occupied and dedicated lives have been lived there. It is a constantly improvised theme which never departed from its own interests or from the appreciation of its own values. The decorations, textiles, pottery, carpets and paintings which fill the rooms are the legacy of fifty years of hard work and enjoyment. Nearly all the decorative commissions of the 1920s were destroyed by bombs during the war and were not replaced. Duncan and Vanessa's sense of colour and their distinctive decorative vocabulary – Vanessa's large lilies or Duncan's mighty-limbed nymphs – do not inspire any modern art students and their canvases have recently received attention only as an interesting side-line of English painting. In so far as the artists had a spokesman for their ideas, Roger Fry filled the post, and Quentin Bell has attempted a summary of his ideas:

> Of the permanent directives which operate upon Fry's thought and actions from the beginning, the first and most important may be indicated by the word *design*: design in the sense of order, intelligence, measure, balance and purpose. For the other I find it harder to discover a word, *social awareness* must serve. He was continually interested in the relationship between art and society even though he was anxious that it should not be overemphasized. The nature of the kind of art that he most admired impelled him to consider its affinities with architecture, decoration and environment.[6]

Vanessa died at Charleston on 7 April 1961 at the age of eighty-one. Duncan was then seventy-six. He continued to paint, exhibit, make new friends, decorate pottery, take an interest in other painters' work and travel: between 1962 and 1974 he visited Spain, Morocco, America, Greece, Cyprus, Portugal and Turkey; at the age of ninety-two he expressed regret, at being told of someone else's visit to Japan, that he had never been to the Far East to see how Oriental artists worked. Duncan died on 8 May 1978, aged ninety-three. The enduring importance of Vanessa and Duncan's near-lifetime of collaboration can be summed up in some notes he once made for a lecture on art: 'The age of the free artist is past; the artist must learn to function under new conditions and above all retain his private vision – which is destroyed by political ideology or moral ideas.'[7]

Notes

CHAPTER 1   pp. 9–40

1   Roger Fry, 'The Last Phase of Impressionism', a letter to the editor, *Burlington Magazine*, March 1908, p. 375.
2   Roger Fry, 'Exhibition of Old Masters at the Grafton Galleries', *Burlington Magazine*, November 1911, p. 71.
3   Roger Fry to G. L. Dickinson, Durbins, 24 September 1910. *Letters*, p. 336.
4   Roger Fry, *Vision and Design*, 1920, p. 192.
5   Duncan Grant, interviewed by Quentin Bell in 'Duncan Grant at Charleston', a film made by Christopher Mason and shown by the BBC in 1970.
6   Leonard Woolf, *Beginning Again*, 1964, p. 27.
7   Roger Fry to Bernard Shaw, 11 December 1912. British Library, Manuscripts Department; quoted by Frances Spalding in *Roger Fry: Art and Life*, 1980, p. 176.
8   Vanessa Bell to Roger Fry, Cleeve House, Wiltshire, August 1912. Charleston Papers.
9   Quoted by Virginia Woolf in *Roger Fry*, 1940, p. 110.
10   ibid., p. 117.
11   William Rothenstein, *Men and Memories*, 1932, p. 219.
12   Vanessa Bell to Clive Bell, 46 Gordon Square, 26 December 1912. Charleston Papers.
13   Roger Fry to G. L. Dickinson, Durbins, 31 May 1913. *Letters*, p. 369.
14   Roger Fry to Lady Fry, Durbins, 14 June 1913. *Letters*, pp. 370–71.
15   Winifred Gill to Duncan Grant, undated (1966–67). Tate Gallery Archives, London.
16   *The Times*, 10 December 1913.

17   Unsigned, undated letter in the papers of C. R. Ashbee. King's College Library, Cambridge. By kind permission of Miss Felicity Ashbee.
18   Omega Workshops catalogue in the Victoria and Albert Museum, London, undated (1915?).
19   Quoted by Quentin Bell and Stephen Chaplin in 'The Ideal Home Rumpus', *Apollo*, October 1964, p. 285.
20   Vanessa Bell to Roger Fry, 46 Gordon Square, 13 October 1913. Charleston Papers.
21   Henri Gaudier-Brzeska, *The Egoist*, 15 June 1914.
22   Roger Fry to Lady Fry, Durbins, 14 December 1913. *Letters*, p. 375.
23   Vanessa Bell to Clive Bell, 46 Gordon Square, 2 April 1912. Charleston Papers.
24   Quentin Bell, 'The Omega Revisited', *Listener*, 30 January 1964, p. 200.
25   Raymond Mortimer, *Duncan Grant*, 1944, p. 9.
26   Roger Fry to Vanessa Bell, Durbins, 24 November 1918. *Letters*, p. 438.
27   Vanessa Bell to Roger Fry, 46 Gordon Square, 24 October 1913. Charleston Papers.
28   Vanessa Bell to Roger Fry, spring 1914. Charleston Papers.

CHAPTER 2   pp. 49–59

1   Letter from Lytton Strachey to a friend, 1 July 1905. Quoted in Michael Holroyd, *Lytton Strachey*, I, 1967, p. 105. By kind permission of the Strachey Trust.
2   Virginia Stephen to Elinor Monsell, Playden, Sussex, 22 September 1907. *Letters*, I, p. 310.
3   Roger Fry to Helen Fry, Brusa, Anatolia, 15 April 1911. *Letters*, pp. 347–48.

4 Vanessa Bell to Roger Fry, 46 Gordon Square, 6 July 1911. Charleston Papers.

5 Virginia Stephen to Vanessa Bell, Little Talland House, Firle, 22(?) August 1911. *Letters*, I, p. 475.

6 Vanessa Bell to Roger Fry, 46 Gordon Square, 25(?) June 1912. Charleston Papers.

7 Vanessa Bell to Roger Fry, 46 Gordon Square, 26(?) June 1912. Charleston Papers.

8 Roger Fry to McKnight Kauffer, Durbins, 5 April 1918. *Letters*, p. 426.

9 Roger Fry to Vanessa Bell, 1912(?). *Letters*, p. 357.

10 Roger Fry to Vanessa Bell, Durbins, 15 September 1912. Charleston Papers.

11 Vanessa Bell to Roger Fry, Asheham, 11 September 1912. Charleston Papers.

12 Vanessa Bell to Clive Bell, 46 Gordon Square, 27 December 1912. Charleston Papers.

13 Vanessa Bell to Roger Fry, 46 Gordon Square, 1914(?). Charleston Papers.

14 Roger Fry to Vanessa Bell, August 1914(?). Charleston Papers.

15 Vanessa Bell to Clive Bell, train to Brandon, August 1913. Charleston Papers.

16 Vanessa Bell to Clive Bell, 46 Gordon Square, 16 August 1913. Charleston Papers.

17 Virginia Woolf to Vanessa Bell, Hogarth House, 16 February 1919. *Letters*, II, p. 331.

18 Vanessa Bell to Roger Fry, Asheham, 17 September 1914. Charleston Papers.

19 Roger Fry to Vanessa Bell, Durbins, 27 February 1915. *Letters*, p. 383.

20 Roger Fry to Clive Bell, Hotel Pas de Calais, Paris, 9 May 1915. *Letters*, p. 385.

CHAPTER 3   pp. 60–71

1 Vanessa Bell to Roger Fry, Asheham, autumn(?) 1914. Charleston Papers.

2 Vanessa Bell to Roger Fry, Eleanor, 1915. Charleston Papers.

3 Nina Hamnett, *Laughing Torso*, 1932, pp. 66–67.

4 Vanessa Bell to Roger Fry, 46 Gordon Square, May 1915. Charleston Papers.

5 Virginia Woolf to Vanessa Bell, Asheham, 16 August 1916. *Letters*, II, p. 111.

6 Vanessa Bell to Roger Fry, 46 Gordon Square, July 1915. Charleston Papers.

7 Vanessa Bell to Roger Fry, Charleston, autumn 1916. Charleston Papers.

8 Vanessa Bell to Clive Bell, Eleanor, April 1915(?). Charleston Papers.

9 Vanessa Bell to Roger Fry, 46 Gordon Square, 25 June 1915. Charleston Papers.

10 Vanessa Bell to Roger Fry, The Grange, Bosham, 6 August 1915. Charleston Papers.

11 Lytton Strachey, quoted in Michael Holroyd, *Lytton Strachey*, I, 1967, p. 25. By kind permission of the Strachey Trust.

12 David Garnett, *The Golden Echo*, II, 1956, p. 123.

13 Vanessa Bell to Roger Fry, Wissett Lodge, end of April 1916. Charleston Papers.

14 Vanessa Bell to Roger Fry, Wissett Lodge, July 1916. Charleston Papers.

15 ibid.

16 Roger Fry to Charles Vildrac, 33 Fitzroy Square, 17 February 1916. *Letters*, p. 393.

17 Roger Fry to Vanessa Bell, Bosham, 5 August 1916. *Letters*, p. 400.

18 Vanessa Bell to Roger Fry, Wissett Lodge, 17 August 1916. Charleston Papers.

19 Roger Fry to Vanessa Bell, 21 Fitzroy Street, 15 June 1916. *Letters*, p. 398.

20 Virginia Woolf to Katherine Cox, Hogarth House, 25 June 1916. *Letters*, II, p. 103.

CHAPTER 4   pp. 72–102

1   Roger Fry, 'The Artist as Decorator',
    Colour, April 1917, pp. 92–93.
2   Roger Fry to Vanessa Bell, 21
    Fitzroy Street, 20 September 1916.
    Charleston Papers.
3   Roger Fry to Lady Fry, Aldbourne,
    Wiltshire, 22 September 1916.
    Letters, pp. 402–03.
4   Roger Fry to Vanessa Bell, 21
    Fitzroy Street, 6 October 1916.
    Charleston Papers.
5   Roger Fry to Vanessa Bell, 21
    Fitzroy Street, 19 March 1917.
    Letters, pp. 406–07.
6   Roger Fry to Vanessa Bell, 21
    Fitzroy Street, 6 March 1917.
    Charleston Papers.
7   Roger Fry, 'An Essay in Aesthetics',
    Vision and Design, 2nd ed., 1925,
    p. 20. First published in *New
    Quarterly*, 1909.
8   Roger Fry to Pamela Fry, 21
    Fitzroy Street, 7 March 1917.
    Letters, p. 406.
9   Vanessa Bell to Roger Fry,
    Charleston, autumn 1916.
    Charleston Papers.
10 David Garnett, *The Golden Echo*,
    II, 1956, p. 125.
11 Vanessa Bell to Roger Fry,
    Charleston, late 1916. Charleston
    Papers.
12 Vanessa Bell to Roger Fry,
    Charleston, March 1917.
    Charleston Papers.
13 Vanessa Bell to Roger Fry,
    Charleston, spring 1917.
    Charleston Papers.
14 Virginia Woolf to Violet Dickinson,
    Asheham, 10 April 1917. *Letters*, II,
    p. 147.
15 Virginia Woolf to Lady Robert
    Cecil, Asheham, 14 April 1917.
    Letters, II, p. 149.
16 Vanessa Bell to Roger Fry, Wissett
    Lodge, 10 May 1916. Charleston
    Papers.
17 Vanessa Bell to Roger Fry, Wissett
    Lodge, July/August 1916.
    Charleston Papers.
18 Quoted by John Rothenstein, in

19 *Modern English Painters*, II, 1956,
    p. 60.
    Roger Fry to Vanessa Bell, Durbins,
    6 April 1917. *Letters*, p. 408.
20 Vanessa Bell to Roger Fry,
    Charleston, 3 August 1917.
    Charleston Papers.
21 Vanessa Bell to Roger Fry,
    Charleston, 21 September 1917.
    Charleston Papers.
22 Virginia Woolf to Lady Ottoline
    Morrell, Asheham, 15 August 1917.
    Letters, II, p. 174.
23 Roger Fry to Vanessa Bell, Durbins,
    16 September 1917. *Letters*,
    pp. 415–16.
24 Clive Bell to Vanessa Bell,
    Garsington, January(?) 1917.
    Charleston Papers.
25 Virginia Woolf to Vanessa Bell,
    Hogarth House, 18 May 1919.
    Letters, II, p. 357.
26 Vanessa Bell to Roger Fry,
    Charleston, winter 1917. Charleston
    Papers.
27 Vanessa Bell to Virginia Woolf,
    Charleston, 13 February 1918.
    Berg Collection, The New York
    Public Library.
28 Clive Bell to Vanessa Bell,
    Garsington, 1918–19. Charleston
    Papers.
29 Roger Fry to Vanessa Bell, Durbins,
    30 July 1918. *Letters*, p. 431.
30 Roger Fry to Vanessa Bell, Durbins,
    22 February 1919. *Letters*, p. 447.
31 Roger Fry to Vanessa Bell, 21
    Fitzroy Street, 11 March 1919.
    Letters, p. 448.
32 Virginia Woolf to Roger Fry,
    Hogarth House, 2 November 1919.
    Letters, II, p. 396.
33 Virginia Woolf, *Roger Fry*, 1940,
    p. 218.

CHAPTER 5   pp. 103–112

1   Virginia Woolf to Saxon Sydney-
    Turner, Asheham, 30 May 1919.
    Letters, II, p. 363.
2   Virginia Woolf to Violet Dickinson,
    Hogarth House, 8(?) May 1919.
    Letters, II, p. 355.

3   Virginia Woolf to Vanessa Bell, Asheham, 21 December 1918. *Letters*, II, pp. 306–07.

4   Clive Bell to Vanessa Bell, Au Voltaire, Paris, 2nd week of November 1919. Charleston Papers.

5   Clive Bell to Vanessa Bell, Au Voltaire, Paris, 27 November 1919. Charleston Papers.

6   Vanessa Bell to Roger Fry, Rome, 11 April 1920. Charleston Papers.

7   Virginia Woolf to Barbara Bagenal, Monks House, 30 December 1921. *Letters*, II, p. 497.

8   Virginia Woolf to Jacques Raverat, 52 Tavistock Square, 5 February 1925. *Letters*, III, p. 164.

9   'Modern Decorative Art – II', *Architectural Review*, November 1925, p. 181.

10 They decorated Angus Davidson's flat at 3 Heathcote Street in 1924; L. A. Harrison's house, Moon Hall in Surrey, in 1925; Raymond Mortimer's flat at 6 Gordon Place in 1925; Nan Hudson and Ethel Sands' 'Garden Room' at the Chateau d'Auppegard near Dieppe in 1927; and Lady Dorothy Wellesley's dining room at Penns-in-the-Rocks, Sussex, between 1928 and 1932. Their only other interior commission before the Second World War was for Ethel Sands' house in Chelsea Square in 1938.

11 Undated notes for a talk on 'cross stitch' to be read at Lewes Art Society. Duncan Grant's Papers.

12 Ronald Grierson to the author, London, 17 February 1979.

13 Raymond Mortimer, *Duncan Grant*, 1944, pp. 13–14.

CHAPTER 6   pp. 129–140

1   Virginia Woolf to Vanessa Bell, Hogarth House, 13 November 1921. *Letters*, II, p. 491.

2   Roger Fry to Helen Anrep, Charleston, 18 April 1925. *Letters*, p. 564.

3   Virginia Woolf to Vanessa Bell, Hogarth House, 20 February 1922. *Letters*, II, p. 506.

4   Vanessa Bell to Virginia Woolf, Villa Corsica, Cassis, 5 February 1927. Berg Collection, The New York Public Library.

5   Virginia Woolf to V. Sackville-West, Villa Corsica, 5 April 1927. *Letters*, III, p. 358.

6   Virginia Woolf to Vanessa Bell, Sicily, 14 April 1927. *Letters*, III, p. 363.

7   Quoted by Richard Shone in *Duncan Grant – Designer*, 1980, p. 23.

8   William Rothenstein, *Since Fifty*, 1939, p. 227.

9   Quentin Bell, in an interview with the author at Cobbe Place, 29 July 1979.

10 Roger Fry, Omega Workshops catalogue, 1915 (?).

11 Mr Leach to Duncan Grant from Cunard, Liverpool, 21 September 1935. Duncan Grant's Papers.

12 Raymond Mortimer, *Duncan Grant*, 1944, p. 29.

13 Kenneth Clark to Sir Evan Charteris, 5 March 1936. Duncan Grant's Papers.

CHAPTER 7   pp. 141–165

1   Grace Higgens in an interview with the author in Sussex, 30 September 1978.

2   Virginia Woolf to Vanessa Bell, Monks House, 27 December 1928. *Letters*, III, p. 566.

3   Vanessa Bell to Winifred Gill, Charleston, 7 July 1946. Victoria and Albert Museum Library, London.

4   John Rothenstein, *Modern English Painters*, II, 1956, p. 60.

5   Duncan Grant to Clive Bell, Charleston, January 1962. Duncan Grant's Papers.

6   Quentin Bell, *Vision and Design*, 1966, p. 7.

7   Duncan Grant, undated notes for a lecture. Duncan Grant's Papers.

Bibliography

ISABELLE ANSCOMBE and CHARLOTTE GERE *Arts and Crafts in Britain and America*, London (Academy Editions) 1978

Phyllis Barron and Dorothy Larcher, exhibition catalogue, Crafts Study Centre, Bath, 1978

MARTIN BATTERSBY *The Decorative Thirties*, London (Studio Vista) 1969

— *The Decorative Twenties*, London (Studio Vista) 1971

QUENTIN BELL, 'The Omega Revisited', *The Listener*, 30 January 1964, pp. 200–201

— and STEPHEN CHAPLIN, 'The Ideal Home Rumpus', *Apollo*, October 1964, pp. 284–91

— *Virginia Woolf: A Biography*, 2 vol., London (Hogarth Press) 1972

— *Bloomsbury*, London (Futura Publications) 1974

R. F. BISSON *The Sandon Studios Society and the Arts*, Liverpool (Parry Books) 1965

X. MARCEL BOULESTIN *Myself, My Two Countries*, London (Cassell) 1936

— *Ease and Endurance*, London (Home & Van Thal) 1948

RICHARD CORK *Vorticism and Abstract Art in the First Machine Age*, London (Gordon Fraser) 1975

H. S. EDE *Savage Messiah*, London (Heinemann) 1939

ROGER FRY *Omega Workshops catalogue*, London, n.d. (1915?). Victoria and Albert Museum Library, London

— *Vision and Design*, London (Chatto & Windus) 1920

— *Duncan Grant*, London (Hogarth Press) 1923

— *Transformations*, London (Chatto & Windus) 1926

— *Cézanne*, London (Hogarth Press) 1927

— *Last Lectures*, Cambridge University Press, 1939

— *The Letters of Roger Fry*, ed. Denys Sutton, London (Chatto & Windus) 1972

MADGE GARLAND *The Indecisive Decade*, London (Macdonald) 1968

PHILIPPE GARNER, ed. *The Phaidon Encyclopaedia of Decorative Arts, 1890–1940*, Oxford (Phaidon) 1978

DAVID GARNETT *The Golden Echo*, London (Chatto & Windus) 1955

— *The Flowers of the Forest*, London (Chatto & Windus) 1956

— *The Familiar Faces*, London (Chatto & Windus) 1962

Duncan Grant – Designer, ed. RICHARD SHONE and JUDITH COLLINS, exhibition catalogue, Bluecoat Gallery, Liverpool, 1980

NINA HAMNETT *Laughing Torso*, London (Constable) 1932

MICHAEL HOLROYD *Lytton Strachey: A Critical Biography*, 2 vol., London (Heinemann) 1967–68

ENID HUWS JONES *Margery Fry: The Essential Amateur*, Oxford University Press, 1966

RICHARD MORPHET, 'The Significance of Charleston', *Apollo*, November 1967, pp. 342–45

RAYMOND MORTIMER *Duncan Grant*, Harmondsworth (Penguin Books) 1944

Paul Nash as a Designer, exhibition catalogue, Victoria and Albert Museum, London, 1975

NIKOLAUS PEVSNER, 'Omega', *Architectural Review*, August 1941, pp. 45–48

RONALD PICKVANCE, 'Duncan Grant and His World', *Apollo*, November 1964, p. 409.

JOHN ROTHENSTEIN *Modern English Painters*, II, London (Eyre and Spottiswoode) 1956

WILLIAM ROTHENSTEIN *Men and*

Memories, 2 vol., London (Faber and Faber) 1931–32
— *Since Fifty*, London (Faber and Faber) 1939
RICHARD SHONE *The Berwick Church Paintings*, Eastbourne (Towner Art Gallery) 1969
— *Bloomsbury Portraits*, Oxford (Phaidon) 1976
ALASTAIR SMART, 'Roger Fry and Early Italian Art', *Apollo*, April 1966, p. 262–71
FRANCES SPALDING *Roger Fry: Art and Life*, London (Granada Publishing) 1980
DENYS SUTTON, 'Omega Revisited', *Financial Times*, 26 November 1963, p. 24
— 'Jacques Copeau and Duncan Grant', *Apollo*, August 1967, pp. 138–41
The Thirties, exhibition catalogue, Arts Council of Great Britain, 1979
DOROTHY TODD and RAYMOND MORTIMER *The New Interior Decoration*, London (Batsford) 1929
PALMER WHITE *Poiret*, London (Studio Vista) 1973
LEONARD WOOLF *Beginning Again*, London (Hogarth Press) 1964
— *Downhill All the Way*, London (Hogarth Press) 1967
VIRGINIA WOOLF *Roger Fry: A Biography*, London (Hogarth Press) 1940
— *The Letters of Virginia Woolf*, 6 vol., London (Hogarth Press) 1975–80
— *The Diary of Virginia Woolf*, 2 vol., London (Hogarth Press) 1977–78

UNPUBLISHED SOURCES

Charleston Papers, in the Archives of the Tate Gallery, London, Acc. no. 8010. (Consulted by kind permission of Angelica Garnett and Quentin Bell. When I read these papers they were in King's College Library, Cambridge, and I would like to thank the Librarian, Mr P. J. Croft, for his kind assistance. The Tate Gallery acquired the correspondence between Roger Fry and Vanessa Bell, Clive and Vanessa Bell and Roger Fry and Clive Bell in July 1980.)
VANESSA BELL, unpublished essays: 'Life at Hyde Park Gate', 'Memories of Roger Fry', 'Notes on Virginia's Childhood', 'Old Bloomsbury' (by kind permission of Angelica Garnett)
PAMELA DIAMAND, *Recollections of Roger Fry and the Omega* (by kind permission of the author)
DUNCAN GRANT, letters and papers (by kind permission of Henrietta Partridge)
WINIFRED GILL, letters to Duncan Grant (by kind permission of Henrietta Partridge. Photocopies on microfilm in the Tate Gallery Archives)
VIRGINIA WOOLF and VANESSA BELL, letters, in the Henry W. and Albert A. Berg Collection, The New York Public Library, Astor, Lenox and Tilden Foundations (by kind permission of the Library)

Acknowledgments

Our thanks first and foremost to Angelica Garnett and Professor and Mrs Quentin Bell for their hospitality and help. We would then like to thank all those who have talked with us, allowed us to photograph in their homes, answered our questions and added to our knowledge: Sir Frederick Ashton, Barbara Bagenal, Lord Clark, Judith Collins, Pamela Diamand, Madge Garland, Philippe Garner, Charlotte Gere, Marina Henderson, Grace Higgens, Sir Geoffrey Keynes, Trekkie Parsons, Henrietta Partridge, Dr George Rylands, Richard Shone and Edward Wolfe; we are also indebted to the late Raymond Mortimer. For help of a more practical nature we would also like to thank Alfred Grey, Richard Holt and Lilian Stevenson.

For the illustrations, our gratitude goes to the following for allowing us access to their houses or collections: Barbara Bagenal *33, 45*; Quentin Bell *34, 50, 51*; Lord Clark *49*; Gallery 25 *28*; Angelica Garnett, Charleston *II, VI, VIII, IX, XIV–XIX*, *24* (plate and dish), *35, 53, 56, 63, 80, 82–84, p.40*; The Hogarth Press *57–62, p.110*; John Jesse *24* (jug), *46*; Dan Klein Ltd *18*; Trekkie Parsons *X, XII*; Richard Shone *48*; The University of Sussex, Monks House *XI, 64–66*; Victoria and Albert Museum, London *III, IV, VII, XIII, 1, 5–11, 15, 16, 19, 20, 22, 23, 42–44, 52, 54, pp.26, 29, 59, 63–65, 71*; Private Collections *V, 47*.

Photographs not by Howard Grey are due to: Quentin Bell and Angelica Garnett *31, 67–78*; Bildarchiv der Österreichischen Nationalbibliothek, Vienna *30*; Courtauld Institute of Art, University of London *21, 25, 26*; Pamela Diamand *12, 29*; Glasgow University, Mackintosh Collection *27*; Grace Higgens *81*; Sotheby Parke Bernet & Co. *I*; Victoria and Albert Museum, London (Crown Copyright) *Frontispiece, 2–4, 13, 14, 17, 40, 41, 55*.

Index

Numbers in *italic* type refer to illustrations